Best wishes,
Paula Rodenas

Best Wishes!
Rita Trapani

Jay Trager
Keep loving horses

The Random House Book of
HORSES and HORSEMANSHIP

The Random House Book of
H·O·R·S·E·S
and
HORSEMANSHIP

By PAULA RODENAS

WITH A FOREWORD BY WALTER FARLEY

Drawings by JEAN CASSELS

Random House / New York

*For Jeanine and all children
who love animals*

— P. R.

I'd like to give sincere thanks to: Kathleen Fallon of the American Horse Shows Association; Fiona Baan of the United States Equestrian Team; Bill Landsman; Anne Elwell of the United States Icelandic Horse Federation; Dana Winslow of Long Island Riding for the Handicapped; Maureen, Ken, and Karissa Kleiman of the Humane Organization for Retired Standardbred Equines; Chuck Grant; Fred Brill of KLM; Leonard C. Hale, Steve Schwartz, Shirley Smith, Karen Downey, Sue Morris Finley, and Charlotte Riggio of the New York Racing Association; Arthur Cussell; my Icelandic friends Reynir Hjartarsson, Magnus Sigmundsson, Baddi Gudlaugsson, and Einar Bollason; Pilar Vico, Francisco Girón Tena, Antonio Alonso, and Antonio Armero Alcántara; Rebecca Lloyd; and my faithful editors Melinda Luke and Stephanie Spinner.

Designed by Jane Byers Bierhorst.

Photograph credits are found on page 180.

*Library of Congress
Cataloging-in-Publication Data:*
Rodenas, Paula.
The Random House book of horses and
horsemanship/by Paula Rodenas ;
with a foreword by Walter Farley.
    p.   cm. Bibliography: p.
Includes index.
SUMMARY: Discusses aspects of horsemanship
and the care of horses.
   ISBN: 0-394-88705-0;
—ISBN 0-394-98705-5 (lib. bdg.)
   1. Horses—Juvenile literature.
2. Horsemanship—Juvenile literature.
[1. Horses.   2. Horsemanship]
I. Title.   II. Title:
Book of horses and horsemanship.
SF302.R63 1991 636.1—dc20 86-42934

Manufactured in Singapore
10 9 8 7 6 5 4 3 2 1

CONTENTS

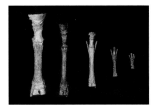
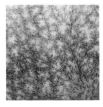

Foreword

I have been writing the Black Stallion books and other horse stories for over 30 years. If it has not made me a professional horseman, I feel justified in thinking that I am a professional observer of horses and the horsemanship of those men, women, and children engaged in the business of training them. My research for story material has taken me all over the world, anywhere people work with horses—from 4-H and Pony Clubs to major racetracks, from show rings to circus rings, from haute école to open jumping and combined training—all places that can be visited in Paula Rodenas's wonderful book. She will introduce you to all kinds of horses and all kinds of people who, despite the different work they do, exemplify the art of horsemanship.

The world of horses is becoming more diverse and specialized each year. For the young equestrian enthusiast it can be a confusing and often baffling world to break into. This clear and thoughtful book provides good, ground-level information for the novice and satisfying reading for the more experienced horse lover.

Yet when all the books have been read and reread, it boils down to the horse, his human companion, and what goes on between them. Many professional horsemen scoff at anything that resembles a sentimental relationship between horse and rider. Yet I have heard these same men admit countless times that horses perform better for some people than others. They're apt to attribute it to anything but what I think it is—*love*. Whatever you wish to label it, it has to do with feeling and understanding between two identities, a sensitivity that cannot be described in so many words (or falsely cultivated). But it is there, always there, if you have the patience and heart to find it.

WALTER FARLEY
Venice, Florida

The Random House Book of
HORSES and HORSEMANSHIP

Cave painting, Lascaux.

I

THE HORSE

Evolution and History

A Tiny Tooth

In 1838 a brickmaker named William Colchester unearthed a tiny tooth while digging for clay in Suffolk, England. He showed the fossil tooth to scientists, but they were unable to identify the animal it belonged to. Years later, when a jaw fragment, a skull, and more teeth were discovered, the mystery of the tiny tooth was finally solved. Scientists agreed that the fossils were the 50-million-year-old remains of the oldest known member of the horse family. They called this prehistoric creature *Eohippus,* which means "dawn horse."

By reconstructing skeletons and parts of skeletons scientists have been able to trace the development of the horse from *Eohippus* to the modern-day horse, *Equus.* This evolution was a slow process that began over 50 million years ago and isn't over yet.

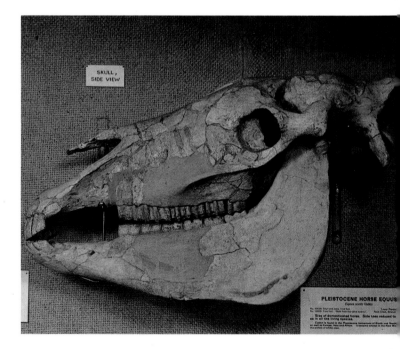

The skull of a Pleistocene Epoch horse, approximately two million years old.

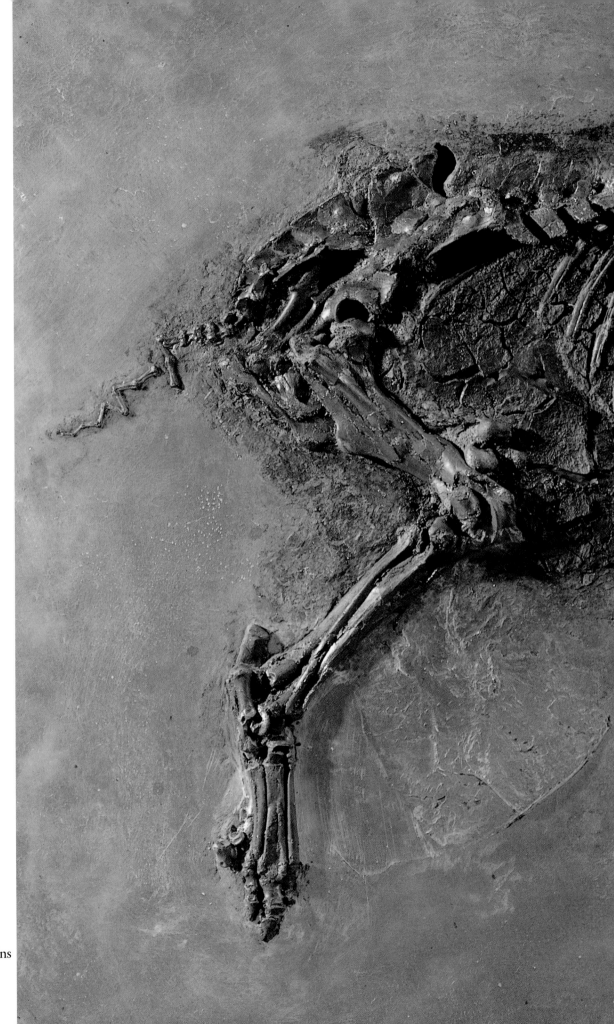

The fossilized remains
of the prehistoric
"dawn horse."

The Evolutionary Journey

Prehistoric *Eohippus* roamed the earth long before the first human being appeared. Unlike today's horse, *Eohippus* was small, no bigger than a fox. He had several toes with soft pads on each foot, which were better suited to traveling on marshy land than running for speed. And so rather than flee from danger, little *Eohippus* was more likely to cower and hide among the lush tropical foliage he browsed on than to bolt in the open.

Nearly 10 million years later (about 40 million years ago) *Eohippus* had evolved into *Mesohippus*. Now the size of a large dog, *Mesohippus* was still small enough to hide from danger among the plants he browsed on. By now *Mesohippus* had lost a toe on each front foot and had developed a larger, stronger middle toe on which to travel, but he was still a relatively slow-moving creature and could not flee from danger.

During the next 18 million years the earth's climate and surface slowly changed and the warm, lush forests became dry, grassy plains. The evolving horse adapted to the changes in order to survive. A new creature in the lineage of the horse appeared—*Merychippus*. His teeth could grind down the tough grasses that were his new food supply, and *Merychippus* had a longer neck to help him reach the grasses. Although *Merychippus* was still multitoed, he carried his weight on a central toe that ended in a hoof. These extra toes would disappear (because they were no longer needed on the plains) after millions of years and were nearly invisible by the time of *Pliohippus*, who lived at the beginning of the ice age about a million years ago.

Pliohippus ran on his strong, blunt middle

Mesohippus   Merychippus

toe—now a hoof. He was swift-footed and could gallop across the plains on which he grazed. This donkey-sized horse also had better vision than his ancestors. Because his eyes were set farther apart on his head, *Pliohippus* could see behind as well as in front. This allowed him to spot danger from all sides while he was grazing. With *Pliohippus* an evolutionary pattern had emerged—the horse of the future would rely on speed for survival.

Reminders of the many soft toes that *Eohippus* and his descendants once traveled on remain as splint bones which run alongside the cannon bones on the modern horse's legs. Unlike his ancestors, today's horse, *Equus,* is built for speed, adapted for grazing, and bigger than ever. Often selectively bred, he is refined and more specialized for his work. Thanks to modern medicine, he is also better equipped for survival than most of his ancestors.

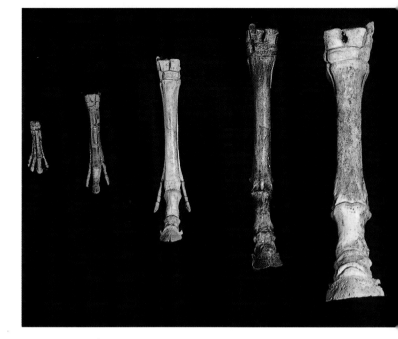

From *Eohippus* to *Equus*—the evolution of the hoof.

Pliohippus

Equus

Humans and the Horse

We know that prehistoric man probably hunted the horse as a source of meat because cave paintings dating back to the Ice Age show hunters and their equine prey. But no one is really sure when horses were first domesticated, although there is evidence that Eurasian nomads first bred and tamed them in captivity around 2500 B.C. From that time on the horse became man's constant companion and an indispensable part of his society. Horses were beasts of burden and a means of transportation. They pulled chariots into battle and plows across the fields. They were featured in art, were bred for economic gain, participated in sports, and soon became a status symbol.

As early as 900 B.C. the Assyrian horse had become an efficient tool in battle, and a new military concept was born: the cavalry. With the existence of the cavalry horsemanship became a desirable skill, since success—not to mention survival—depended on the abilities of the mounted troops.

Horsemanship played an important part in the life of the ancient Greeks, whose first Olympic games, in the eighth century B.C., featured horse racing and other horse sports. The Greeks were also the first culture to appreciate riding as an art form. The historian and essayist Xenophon, who wrote about the care, breeding, and riding of horses in the fourth or fifth century B.C., is still read today, and his enlightened teachings form the basis of good modern horse training. Xenophon urged that the horse always be treated with kindness rather than force:

> For what a horse does under constraint . . . he does without understanding, and with no more grace than a dancer would show if he were whipped and goaded. Under such treatment horse and man alike will do much more that is ugly than graceful.
>
> —Xenophon, "The Art of Horsemanship," *Scripta Minora*

During the time that Xenophon was writing, there were no horses at all on the American continents. *Eohippus* and his descendants had long before migrated across land bridges to Europe and Asia. When the land bridges later disappeared under the oceans, the primitive horses were unable to come back. It wasn't until the 16th century that horses returned with the Spanish conquistadors, and remained to play a pivotal role in the settlement of the New World.

The Indians of the New World soon acquired horses and became expert riders, using horses for mounted warfare, for hunting game, and as pack animals. During the American Revolution the United States Cavalry was formed. Subsequently, cavalry horses went into battle in the Mexican War, the Civil War, and the Indian wars. Mounted troops were largely responsible for settling the western portions of the United States.

The demand for cattle in the American West during the late 1800s helped to create a romantic hero—the cowboy. Horses and cowboys herded thousands of cattle across the country in cattle drives, and news and mail moved via the Pony Express. Modern cowboys still work on horseback with cattle today the way the early cowboys did during the last century.

By World War II the horse was no longer a primary means of transportation. The automobile had replaced horse-drawn wagons and carriages. Teamsters no longer drove teams of horses—they drove trucks. Tractors replaced horses in front of the plow. In 1950 the U.S. Cavalry disbanded, and the horse was relieved

A Pony Express rider on his way from
Missouri to California.

Horses played an important role in
the culture of the American Indian,
allowing some of the tribes to live a
nomadic existence.

The Round-Up, by Frederic
Remington. Cowboys, Indians,
and other Western subjects figured
prominently in the work of this well-
known 19th-century artist.

The United States mail was carried by
horse and stagecoach, as shown in this
19th-century engraving.

of his duties on the battlefield. The age of the horse was over—or so it seemed.

But the bond between human beings and the horse proved to be of such strength that the past few decades have seen an astonishing revival of interest in horses. Now that bond transcends the utilitarian partnership of the past. No longer serving in the workaday world, the horse has become a means of recreation and sport for an increasing number of people each year. It is a tribute to this beautiful and versatile creature that the horse is thriving in its new role. Today there are more horses in this country than there were at the turn of the century.

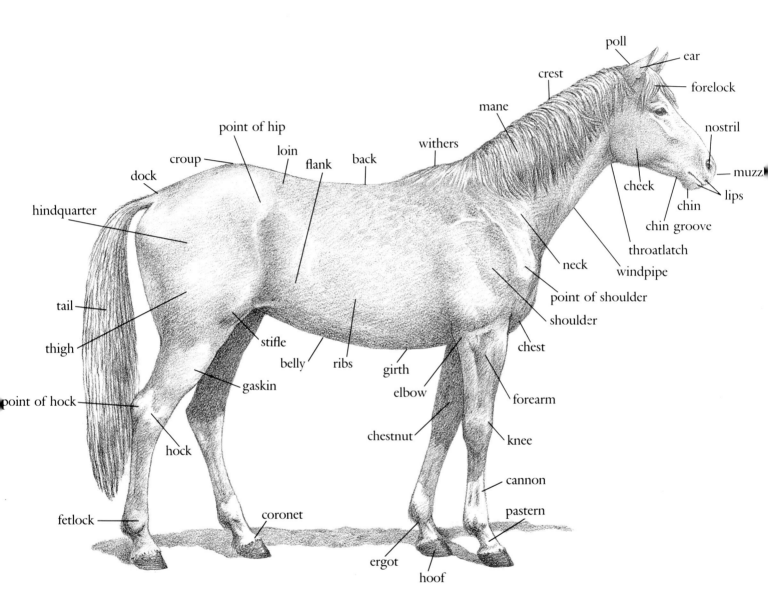

poll

ear

crest

forelock

mane

nostril

point of hip

withers

muzz[le]

loin

cheek

croup

flank

back

lips

dock

chin

hindquarter

chin groove

neck

throatlatch

windpipe

tail

point of shoulder

thigh

shoulder

stifle

chest

point of hock

belly

ribs

girth

gaskin

elbow

forearm

hock

chestnut

knee

cannon

fetlock

coronet

pastern

ergot

hoof

II

ANATOMY AND BEHAVIOR

The Points of the Horse

Horsemen often sound as if they speak a different language than the rest of the world. To the inexperienced person a horse with upright pasterns, high withers, or a frog in its hoof is a bewildering creature indeed! Understanding the points of the horse (which is really to say "the parts of the horse") is the first step in learning about horses.

Anatomy

Nature has provided the horse with a body designed for speed. Strongly muscled hindquarters help him to push off rapidly from a standstill and, with his long, slender legs and hooves, to cover ground quickly. A deep chest accommodates a large heart and lungs, essential for speed and endurance. And his long neck helps the horse keep his balance while in motion.

The horse has keen senses. He will often turn his head and ears in the direction of a distant sound, detecting it long before a human can. The horse's vision extends around to his sides, so that he can take in a panoramic view of his surroundings. Most sensitive is the horse's sense of smell. A healthy horse can detect a mare in season, identify familiar animals or people, or detect an intruder with its superior sense of smell. All of his senses enable the horse to hear, see, and sniff out potential danger, and his anatomy allows him to transform danger signals into flight.

The Hoof

There is an old saying among horsemen: "No foot, no horse." Hooves must be broad and well matched, for they absorb most of the shock of the horse's movement. Because the walls of the hoof are continually growing, they need regular trimming and filing (much as human nails do).

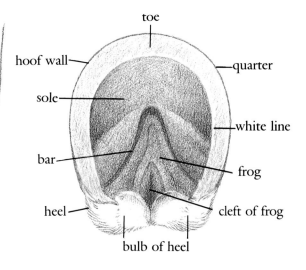

coronet

toe

hoof wall

quarter

sole

white line

bar

frog

heel

cleft of frog

bulb of heel

How Horses Are Measured

Horses are measured in "hands," one hand being equal to four inches (10 centimeters). Measurement is taken at the highest point of the withers. Therefore a horse that measures 16 hands is 64 inches (1.6 meters) tall at the withers. The measuring is done with a special stick called a *horse measuring standard,* which is held upright next to the horse with a horizontal arm reaching across the withers.

Horses and Ponies

Classification of horses and ponies is easy—most of the time. It is universally accepted that a horse measuring under 14.2 hands (57 inches, or 1.5 meters) at the withers is a pony. By the same token, a larger animal would be a horse. But it isn't always so simple. Many purebred Arabians, for example, are small enough to be considered ponies—but aren't. And many ponies are taller than 14.2 hands but are nonetheless regarded as ponies.

Ponies are characteristically different from horses in several ways. They tend to be hardier and healthier, and they are uniformly considered surefooted, even-tempered, and clever. Icelandic, Welsh, and Shetland ponies, originally beasts of burden, can pull or carry heavy weights for their size. Their coats are rougher than horses', even in mild weather; in cold climates they grow thick, shaggy coats that protect them from damp as well as chilly weather.

Modern ponies are often crossbreeds—Welsh-Thoroughbred or Welsh-Arabian crosses. With their fine bones and smooth coats they closely resemble the purebred Arabian and Thoroughbred.

Although zoologists consider ponies a distinct zoological type, most closely related to primitive horses, it is often hard to say just what is so very different about a horse and a pony.

Colors and Markings

"Any good horse is a good color," a wise horseman once said. Although color does not determine a horse's character or performance, it does affect its appearance. And for today's breeders and buyers, who are often as interested in appearance as they are in strength or speed or endurance, colors and markings are important. The four commonest equine colors are brown (bay), chestnut (sorrel), black, and gray. However, there are many variations of these colors and of patterns (see below).

Colors

Black

Black horses are uniformly black all over.

Brown and Bay

A bay or brown horse may range from a reddish tinge to almost black. Bay horses have a black mane and tail, and their legs are also black. A brown horse may be almost black except for the brownish area around the muzzle and eyes, belly, and insides of the legs or may be any shade of brown with a brown mane and tail.

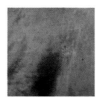

Chestnut and Sorrel

The chestnut or sorrel horse has a brown coat, usually with reddish highlights. The mane and tail either match the coat or are somewhat lighter. The color known as liver chestnut is the darkest of all chestnuts.

Gray

There is a tremendous variety in the colors and shades of gray horses. Born brown or black, they turn dark gray, light gray, and white as they grow. Flea-bitten grays have light-gray coats flecked with darker gray; dappled grays have coats of differing shades of gray that form a circular pattern. And horses that appear to be completely white are almost always grays—the only truly white horses are albinos, whose skin is pink and whose eyes are blue, brown, or hazel.

Dun and Buckskin

The dun is tan or light brown, with a black mane and tail, black markings on its legs, and—unlike its close cousin, the buckskin—a black dorsal stripe running the length of its spine.

Palomino

The Palomino is a golden horse, ideally the color of a newly minted penny. He has a light mane and tail and no dark markings. He may have white below the knees and hocks and white markings on his face, but nowhere else.

Pinto (Also Called Paint)

The Pinto's coloring consists of large patches of black and white (*piebald*) or brown and white (*skewbald*). A Pinto with a dark coat and white patches is called an *overo*. A white horse with dark patches is known as a *tobiano*.

Roan

A roan's basic color of hair is mixed with sprinklings of white. Thus a black or dark brown horse with a mixture of white hairs is called a "blue roan," and a chestnut with white hairs is a "red roan." A light chestnut roan is sometimes known as a "strawberry roan."

Appaloosa

The Appaloosa is known for the different patterns of spots (large and small) that may cover all of his body or just his hindquarters. His coat may be gray, black, chestnut, roan, or brown. The spots may be light or dark. Appaloosas can also be solid colors. They qualify by exhibiting other proper Appaloosa characteristics, such as mottled skin and striped hooves. The Appaloosa is a registered breed.

Markings

While the color of a horse's coat may change with age, the size and shape of his markings will stay the same throughout his lifetime. They are as helpful as fingerprints for the purposes of identification, since no two horses will have both the same color and the same exact markings on the face or legs. Some of the commonest markings are shown below.

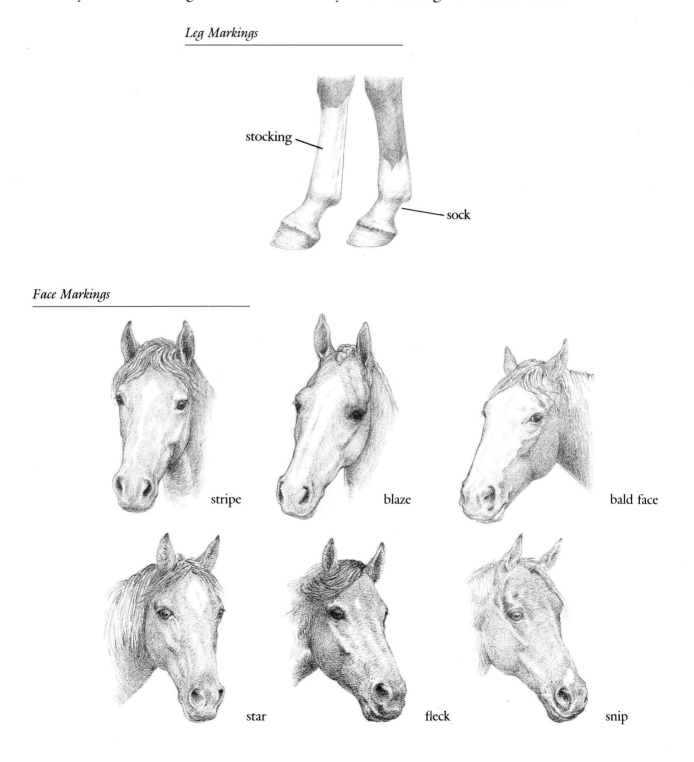

Leg Markings

stocking

sock

Face Markings

stripe

blaze

bald face

star

fleck

snip

The Gaits

> He moved like a dancer, which is not surprising: a horse is a beautiful animal, but it is perhaps most remarkable because it moves as if it always hears music.
>
> — Mark Helprin,
> *Winter's Tale*

Motion is at the very core of the modern horse's being, for his survival has always depended on his efficiency in motion. For horse lovers his beauty and nobility are best expressed by it.

Walk

The walk has four beats, as each of the horse's hooves touches the ground separately. If the horse is walking forward energetically, using his hindquarters to propel his motion, his hind feet will overstep the prints left by his front feet, and he is said to have good *impulsion*.

Trot

The trot is a two-beat gait in which the diagonal (opposite) front and hind feet touch the ground simultaneously.

Canter

Many people think that the canter and gallop differ only in terms of speed, but the canter has three beats and the gallop four. In the canter the horse leads with either his right or his left front leg and is said to be on the right lead or left lead. On the left lead the left hind leg and right front leg hit the ground together and the right hind leg and left front leg hit the ground independently. It is just the opposite for the right lead. When the horse is cantering in a circle, his inside hind leg usually leads, although in advanced training the horse may be asked to perform a counter canter and canter with his outside leg leading.

Walk

Trot

Canter

Gallop

The gallop differs from the canter in that it is a considerably faster, four-beat gait. In a gallop each of the horse's hooves strikes the ground separately, so that a distinct four beats can be heard.

Other Gaits

Some variations on the basic gaits are the rapid walking *tölt* of the Icelandic horse, and the *pacing* of horses that move their left front and left hind legs together, followed by the right front and right hind legs.

Jumping

Although horses do not have the physical ability to jump great heights in relation to their size, selective breeding has produced powerful and athletic jumpers. When the horse jumps, his hindquarters push him off the ground and propel him through the air. As the horse clears a fence his front legs tuck neatly under his body, and at the highest point of the jump his back curves in a graceful arc, or *bascule*. His hind legs bend at the hocks as they follow.

Behavior

The Herd

Horses in the wild live in herds, not just because they want to be with other horses, but because it is safer. A horse living alone cannot always be on the alert for danger. Many horses living together ensures that some will continuously be on the lookout for any threat to the herd. Herd living is also important for maintaining a good natural breeding system for wild horses.

The herding instinct is strong even in domestic horses, who often find the security of the stable a replacement for the herd. Domestic horses are happiest when they live with other horses, but often they are content to have a donkey, a goat, or a pony for a companion.

Wild and domestic horses alike observe a strict "pecking order" within their group. In herds of wild horses the herd leader is often a stallion, but not always. In groups of domestic horses the herd leader is often a gelding or a mare. Usually this horse is first at the hay and the water bucket and is at the front of the group as it moves about the pasture. Oftentimes other horses will follow where it leads.

A horse stretched out on the ground is usually not sick—just relaxing!

Rolling eyes, pinned-back ears, bared teeth, and flared nostrils all say, "Back off!"

This horse's relaxed appearance and curious expression are signs that he is very approachable.

Body Language

Horses communicate their feelings—to humans and to each other—through a complex set of expressions and postures. To an observer who knows horses' body language, an outstretched neck, pinned-back ears, and flared nostrils mean "Watch out if you know what's good for you!" But an arched neck, ears pricked forward, and a relaxed face generally mean "Hi, how's it going?" Curiosity, pleasure, boredom, tension, fear, anger, and aggression are all expressed, though silently, with body language.

A horse's voice, too, can reveal its feelings. Horses call to one another with a whinny. A low, soft nicker is a friendly greeting to another horse or a human friend. Snorts come from anxious or excited horses. Squeals come from horses that are startled or hurt—or flirting. A horse suffering great pain will scream. Blows, sighs, grunts, and groans are all sounds that horses use to communicate with one another and with people. To the informed listener and observer, the horse is a very articulate creature.

Although domestic horses have lost their freedom to roam and graze, they enjoy certain advantages their wild counterparts do not. A domestic horse may feel safe enough to sleep stretched out on the ground, and even snore. A wild horse may only doze on its feet for brief periods each night. Wild horses spend the greater part of each day on the move, grazing for their food. Domestic horses eat regular meals and fill their idle hours with play. When they are happy or feeling good, they will run and buck just for the fun of it. Or they may amuse themselves with nips and tugs on each other's halters. Colts and fillies often perform leaps that seem to defy gravity, while older horses may spend hours grooming each other. Much of what appears to be horseplay is in fact an exercise of the horse's basic instincts: galloping as if from danger, challenging each other like herd leaders, or showing off as in courtship.

Equine behavior is the result of careful planning by nature. Everything the horse is and does has been designed to ensure its continued survival, and comes from centuries of evolutionary improvement.

Even domestic horses have a "herd leader" in the pasture—whose authority might be challenged by a newcomer.

III

BREEDING AND THE LIFE CYCLE

For 50 million years horse breeding was controlled by nature. Beginning with little *Eohippus,* nature experimented with new and better types of animal until it finally produced the modern horse, *Equus.* Survival of the species was the overriding concern of nature-as-breeder. However, now that the horse's continued survival depends less on nature and more on mankind, breeding is nothing short of a science. Today breeding is programmable, predictable, and technological. It may even occur between horses who will never meet. But it begins, as it always has, with a stallion (sire) and a broodmare (dam).

Natural and Selective Breeding Methods

Breeding between horses is of two types—natural (occurring among horses running free) and selective (controlled by breeders).

Natural breeding (or pasture breeding) takes place in the spring, when a stallion breeds within his herd of mares. It is a charged time for the herd. In the wild not only does the stallion need to protect the herd from predators and outside stallions attracted by the mares in season, but he needs to mate with each mare within a relatively short span of time. The resulting foals will then be born 11 months later, at the beginning of the mild season, when the food supply is most plentiful and the climate kinder to babies.

Selective breeding is now the more conventional method for domestic horses. This is a planned mating between a specially selected broodmare and stallion. Although it can occur at any time of year, it still most often happens in the spring.

The breeder selects a stallion and broodmare that he or she thinks will produce a best-quality foal. Breeders study pedigrees (ancestry) and genetic traits such as conformation and racing

A mare being artificially inseminated.

This broodmare's enlarged abdomen shows that she is nearing the end of her pregnancy.

ability—qualities passed along through heredity. Breeders also consider temperament and talent.

If breeding is to occur by natural means, the stallion and mare are brought to an area where they are physically separated by a low partition called a teasing wall. The handlers observe the mare's reaction to the stallion's presence and behavior to determine if she is ready to mate. This procedure is called "teasing." If the mare is ready, mating can proceed.

In the past 10 years or so artificial insemination has become common. This means that the stallion's semen is collected and used to impregnate a mare that lives too far away to be bred to the stallion by natural means. Because semen can be frozen, it can be shipped to almost any part of the world.

Another miracle of modern science is the embryo transfer. The mare is bred, and after nine days the fertilized egg is removed, either surgically or by flushing it out. It is then placed in a "carrier" mare, called a *surrogate;* the embryo (the developing foal) grows inside her uterus and then is normally delivered. This method is costly and not always successful. Its value is that it enables a mare of top quality to produce five or six foals a year instead of just one, or to compete without being slowed down by pregnancy.

The Pregnant Mare

It takes 11 months for the foal embryo to develop in its mother's womb. During this time the mare can be ridden or exercised, although care must be taken so that she doesn't fall and injure herself.

The fetus (developing foal) lies in a bag of water called *amniotic fluid,* which protects it from jarring. It receives nourishment from its

A mare in the birthing position.

mother through the umbilical cord, which joins the foal to the inside of the womb—specifically, to a part called the *placenta,* or afterbirth, which is discarded after the foal is born.

The mare should be fed well and given supplements of vitamins and minerals to nourish her and her foal. She may be put on a high-protein-grain diet. The veterinarian can advise the breeder about diet, exercise, and worming and recommend inoculations to be given during pregnancy and lactation (nursing).

Pregnant mares sometimes behave very differently toward their handlers and other horses than they did before pregnancy. A formerly sweet and tractable mare may become extra alert or suspicious, lazy, or even jealous.

If the pregnancy is not going well, the mare may abort (lose the foal). This often happens when she is carrying twins, because there is rarely enough room for two foals to develop properly.

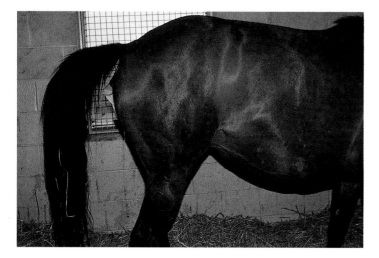

The tips of the foal's front hooves can just be seen emerging from the mother.

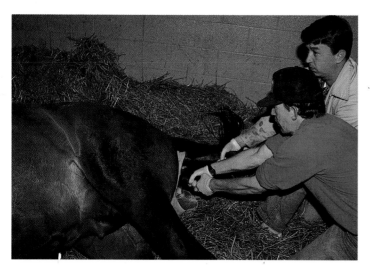

The mare lies down while powerful contractions push the foal from her body. The handlers step in only when necessary.

The hard work is over. The new mother greets her baby!

Birth of a Foal

Spring nights are busy times on breeding farms. Breeders watch their mares carefully for signs that birth is imminent. A mare will sweat, lick her coat, pace nervously in her stall, and, when it is time for the foal to be born, lie on her side. Powerful contractions push the foal out of her body into the world.

Most of the time the birth is normal, and the mare manages very well on her own. One possible complication is a breech birth, when the foal is positioned to come out of the mother hind end first instead of head first and has to be turned around. Since there is usually not enough time to call a vet, most breeders have learned what to do during a breech birth. If the birth is normal, however, the breeder does not interfere. He steps in *after* the umbilical cord has been broken in order to disinfect and tie it. Then he may help the foal to its feet and make sure it gets its first feeding, which contains valuable *colostrum*—the mother's first milk, rich in protein and protective antibodies. He makes sure that the placenta is safely delivered. He watches to see that the foal passes its first manure, so that he knows its digestive system is functioning as it should.

The entire birth may last only 10 to 15 minutes. Most mares take to motherhood so naturally that the breeder may not even be aware that the foal has been born until he wakes up one morning to find it washed, standing, and nursing in its mother's stall!

The Newborn Foal

A healthy newborn foal often stands up on its wobbly legs within 15 minutes after birth. The mare licks the foal clean and dry, and it instinctively sucks its mother's milk. The mare and

When the mare or foal stands for the
first time, the umbilical cord breaks.
Mother and baby get to know each
other as the mare licks her baby clean
and dry. In the next several hours
the foal will get its first drink of
colostrum, which is high in vitamins
and antibodies.

Playful foals can make a game out of almost anything—even chewing their mothers' halters!

The bonds between mare and foal are strong, and difficult to break when foals are weaned at about six months.

foal are usually kept indoors for the first few days. After that, if the weather is good, they may be turned out to pasture during the day.

It is important for the mare and foal to get to know each other in those first days after birth. In the wild this is crucial to survival. Shortly after the mare licks her newborn dry, she learns its smell and will accept no other foal. During the first few days she will not allow any other horse near her foal. In this way her baby becomes so familiar with her that it can recognize her sound, look, and smell.

Once the foal has gained control of its legs, it will follow its mother like a little shadow, galloping at her side in the pasture. If handled gently by humans from birth, it should grow up with a trust in them that will carry over into its training.

Stages of Growth

Horses mature rapidly, often reaching 80 percent of their height in the first year.

At five or six months of age the domestic foal is weaned—separated from its mother. (Foals in the wild may nurse for a year.) No longer receiving its mother's milk, it should be fed carefully to make sure it is neither overfed nor undernourished. Weanlings (foals between six and 12 months of age) are happiest when they have company to take their minds off the separation, and they are often kept together. By the time they reach 12 months (yearling), the colts (male foals) and fillies (female foals) are separated from one another. As a two-year-old, the horse's bones begin to strengthen, and it starts to fill out.

Young horses do well when turned out under good conditions, in a pasture that offers plenty of grass and has an adequate water supply, safe fencing, and good footing. Soil that is rich in certain minerals, such as limestone, phosphorus, nitrogen, potash, and calcium, has a beneficial effect on the development of horses. For that reason certain parts of the world are known to produce superior horses. The Kentucky "bluegrass," the southern part of Spain where Andalusians are bred, and Ireland are world-famous breeding grounds.

Horses are said to be in their prime from the age of seven or eight into the early teens. Some horses live longer than others; ponies usually live to ripe old ages, often past 30, and many horses continue to be useful past the age of 20.

David Gribbons, BREEDER

David Gribbons breeds warmblood sporting horses at the Knoll Farm in Brentwood, New York.

"I grew up on a farm, so I've always had animals around. We used to breed cattle.

"My wife, Anne, is Swedish and an avid dressage competitor. She introduced me to the warmblood breeds. The warmbloods have good bones and sound dispositions, and they're good for dressage. We got into horse breeding when we bought a Trakehner colt, Bagatelle, who was four months old. My wife wanted to ride him eventually, and I wanted to breed him and see if I could produce others like him. It was exciting.

"That was twelve years ago, when breeding was conducted 'naturally'—that is, it was simply a matter of putting the mare and the stallion together and letting nature take its course. It wasn't always successful; horses could get injured or develop infections.

Today it can be done artificially. A stallion at our Knoll Farm in New York can sire a foal in California! It's done through laboratory techniques.

"At one time we had twenty to twenty-five foals born on our property. Now we have only five or six born here each year, because our space is limited. But we breed eighty to a hundred mares a year to our stallions, or about thirty mares per stallion. Breeding has become a part of our business, in addition to our boarding and training stable.

"When a foal is born, I try to be there. When I help it to its feet, it tries to nurse from my fingers, thinking I'm its mother. Anne begins to take an interest later, when the youngsters are ready to be trained and ridden, but in the beginning, I'm the 'mother.' It's a very nice feeling to have a little animal turn to you for love and warmth."

IV

THE BREEDS
OF THE WORLD

Centuries of Change

After centuries of evolutionary improvements, the horse still transforms itself each time it reproduces—hopefully refining, specializing, and strengthening its breed. The combined efforts of human beings and nature have produced hundreds of breeds of horses—some now extinct—with more to come in the future. Breeders today strive for a degree of perfection never before reached in selective breeding, searching for the embodiment of a particular breed. There are more than 150 breeds of horses in the modern world. Here are some of the commonest ones.

Hotbloods, Warmbloods, Coldbloods

These terms do not refer to the actual temperature of any particular horse's blood, but rather to its temperament, or personality. Hotbloods are said to be high-spirited horses and are

A beautiful Andalusian at a horse fair in southern Spain.

generally among the fastest. The Arab and the Thoroughbred are hot-blooded horses. The cold-blooded horses are the large, heavy-boned draft breeds, which are usually quiet, calm, and easy-going. The Clydesdale and Percheron are cold-blooded horses. The warmbloods, as the term suggests, are in many ways a combination of the two—in breeding (they are often cross-breeds) and in temperament. The Trakehner and the Holsteiner are warm-blooded horses.

Breed Registries

Breed registries are established and maintained by organizations and sometimes by countries. They record the names of horses believed worthy of carrying on the desired traits of the breed. In some instances a committee decides on the acceptability of a horse for registry. In others a horse may be registered simply on the basis of his pedigree or his color. Most organizations issue a certificate of registration that is transferred from owner to owner.

Cold-blooded horses still work on some farms, though they are more commonly used for breeding and sport.

The Breeds

Arabian

The Arabian horse is the world's oldest breed. It is also considered by many to be the most beautiful horse in the world. Certainly no other breed has played a more important role in the history of horse breeding.

Arabians are prized for their beauty and performance. Intelligent and sensitive, they are also known for endurance, spirit, and loyalty. Arabians are generally small horses, averaging 14.2 to 15.1 hands. They range from bay, gray, and chestnut to black in color. Their signature feature is a small, refined head with a dish-shaped face.

According to Arab legend, the great Islamic prophet Mohammed once led a herd of horses across the desert for many days without food or water. Just as they reached a watering hole, and the thirsty horses began to drink, an enemy tribe approached. The call to battle was sounded, and all but five of the horses kept on drinking. The five loyal mares who responded to the call were supposedly the foundation mares of the breed.

Although it may be hard to separate legend from reality, we do know that the Arabian horse's breeding can be traced as far back as 1800, and legend follows the breed back to the seventh century B.C. and possibly earlier. Not only did the Arabs maintain pure bloodlines in their horses, they also treated them as members of the family, sharing their food and tents with them.

The hot-blooded Arabian has had a strong influence on other breeds. Its prepotency (ability to transmit its traits to offspring) has left its mark on many of the world's horses.

Thoroughbred

Thoroughbred horses were first recorded as a breed in the British Thoroughbred stud book (registry) in 1793. The origins of the breed can be traced to three Oriental (Arab) foundation sires: the Godolphin Arabian, the Darley Arabian, and the Byerly Turk. Some of the early mares were also of Oriental stock; others were native English mares that showed an aptitude for speed. The Thoroughbred was bred for racing, but proved to have abilities for jumping and dressage (classical training on the flat) as well. (The name of the breed should not be confused with the word "purebred." A pure-bred horse is a horse of any breed with pure bloodlines, whereas the Thoroughbred is a distinct breed in itself.)

The average Thoroughbred is between 15 and 17 hands. He is generally long legged, athletic, fairly short backed, and noble in appearance, sometimes bearing a resemblance to his Arabian ancestors in the shape of his head and face. If there are any weaknesses in the Thoroughbred, they lie in his brittle feet and the fact that some members of the breed are too fine-boned to stand up to the heavy demands of eventing. But of all the horses in the world, the Thoroughbred is most often called the perfect light horse.

lish bloodlines and was bred for short races, usually no longer than a quarter mile—hence the name Quarter Horse.

More muscular and compact than the Thoroughbred, the Quarter Horse's strong hindquarters and quick reflexes enable him to "turn on a dime" and to go rapidly from a halt to a gallop. He may be of any solid color (sometimes Palomino) or roan and averages 15 hands.

Quarter Horses proved strong enough to carry heavy men and packs, yet they were agile and fast. In addition their skill at herding cattle soon made them the obvious choice of the American cowboy for driving, herding, rodeo, and ranch work.

Because they are not only physically adept but also intelligent, Quarter Horses today are used in both English and Western competition as well as racing.

American Quarter Horse

The American Quarter Horse is considered the oldest native American breed. It originated in the American colonies from Spanish and Eng-

Morgan

The foundation sire of the Morgan breed, foaled in 1793 in Massachusetts, was originally named Figure, but he was later given the name of one of his owners, a Vermont schoolteacher called Justin Morgan. Before his death in 1821, the little (14.1-hand) stallion had achieved considerable fame in weight-pulling contests and races by outdoing all his competitors, many of whom were larger than he. He passed on his looks, talent, and stamina to his offspring; many modern Morgan horses still bear a striking resemblance to their distinguished ancestor.

The modern-day Morgan is usually bay, brown, chestnut, liver chestnut, or black. He is still small (from 14 to 15.2 hands) and has a rounded, muscular body and short, sturdy legs. He is best known for his strength, versatility, soundness, and gentle temperament. The breed has been carefully preserved in Vermont, and its popularity has spread to other parts of the United States. For many years the Morgan was the only breed used by the U.S. Army. As a pleasure mount, he is hard to beat. Morgans compete under saddle and in harness, and many are excellent jumpers.

Standardbred

Standardbred horses owe their beginning to a gray Thoroughbred called Messenger, imported in 1788 from England to Philadelphia. Messenger's great-grandson, Hambletonian 10, became a leading sire. The robust breed also includes a mixture of Hackney and Morgan.

Standardbreds are slightly smaller than Thoroughbreds, sturdier of build, and mild tempered. They may be bay, brown, chestnut, black, or gray. They are noted for strong legs and good stamina.

The Standardbred is the fastest breed in harness racing, working as either trotters or pacers. Until recent years it was believed that Standardbreds were unsuited to anything but harness racing, and those that were not fast enough or sound enough, sadly, were destroyed. Certain groups, such as H.O.R.S.E. (Humane Organization for Retired Standardbred Equines), founded in New York at Roosevelt Raceway in 1980, began to encourage putting ex-racers up for adoption and retraining them for riding purposes. Today there are riding and driving classes for Standardbreds around the United States, and many former racing horses have gone on to new ways of life.

American Saddlebred Horse

The high-stepping American Saddlebred Horse owes much of his flamboyant style to the race horse Denmark, foaled in Kentucky in 1839.

Color Breeds

Some horses are special because of their color or their markings. For this reason there are registries for such horses: they include Palomino, Pinto, Appaloosa, and Albino. These horses may be registered with one association for color and another for breed. For example, a Palomino Quarter Horse may be registered as a Quarter Horse with the American Quarter Horse Association and as a Palomino with the Palomino Horse Association.

Appaloosa

The Appaloosa takes its name from the Palouse River in Oregon, home of the Nez Percé Indians, who first bred these horses from Spanish stock. The Appaloosa's spots make him easy to identify. They come in many patterns: leopard, snowflake, blanket, and others. In addition to his striking markings, the Appaloosa is known for stamina and a good disposition. Although they are thought of in the United States as American Indian horses, equines with Appaloosa markings appear in ancient paintings and ceramics from China and Japan.

Palomino

A Palomino has a golden coat with a white or cream mane and tail, making it an extremely eye-catching horse. Palominos are commonly Quarter Horses in the United States but may be other breeds; acceptability of breeds varies from country to country.

Pinto

The Pinto (sometimes called the Paint Horse) differs from the Appaloosa in that his spots are large patches of color. There are two types of Pinto spot patterns: the overo and the tobiano, and two colors: piebald (black and white) and skewbald (brown and white). Pinto coloring may be found in many breeds. American Indians favored Pintos because they had built-in camouflage and bred them in the Western states, probably from Spanish stock.

Albino

With his snow-white coat and pink skin, the Albino is completely without pigmentation (color). Although albino horses may appear at random in any breed, Albinos have been bred and registered in the United States since the 1930s. A foundation stallion called Old King is cited as a leading sire, and it is believed that he had Arabian-Morgan origins. Albinos may have blue, brown, or hazel eyes and may be sensitive to sunlight.

V

HORSE CARE

At one time horses were dependent on their environment and on one another for their well-being and survival. Today most horses rely on human beings each and every day of their lives, beginning at birth. Shelter, food, water, exercise, and medical attention are given to the horse by its caretakers in exchange for whatever "services" the horse offers. Happily, for many horses, the arrangement is a good one.

The Horse at Grass

In the wild, horses live out in the open. So does the domesticated horse that lives outside. This is called being kept "at grass." Horses at grass require enough space to graze and exercise, well-drained land, good-quality grass, safe fencing, and a supply of fresh water. The horse at grass will certainly require less care than the stabled horse, but he shouldn't be left on his own each day. Field-kept horses need daily hoof inspections and should be regularly checked

This horse's low stall door topped with a stall guard permits him to "socialize" in the barn.

A nice-size run-in shed in a well-tended pasture.

The tools of the trade.

for injury. If the pasture grass is nutritionally lacking, food supplements, such as hay, grain, or salt, may be added to the horse's diet.

The Stabled Horse

Most horse owners in colder climates provide some shelter for their horses. The simplest form of shelter is the run-in shed. A rudimentary, three-sided open building in the pasture of field-kept or stabled horses, the run-in shed provides a barrier between horses and severe weather. The horse simply runs in and waits until the weather improves.

Some horse owners are fortunate enough to have a small barn in which to keep their animals. Horses can be turned out into the pasture during the day and stabled at night or turned out for short periods each day. Whatever the situation, the backyard barn must meet certain safety standards. Fire extinguishers should be kept on hand. In the event of a fire, planning ahead for the evacuation of stabled horses may save their lives. Stalls must be free of hazards such as loose nails and boards. Although barns do not require heating, they should provide protection from extremes of heat and cold, drafts, and dampness. Ceilings must be high enough to clear the head of the most curious horse and doorways wide enough so that horses can be led in and out comfortably. Good light, ventilation, and running water are essential, and so is a clean, dry area for feed and hay storage. A tack room, although not essential, is an added convenience. The manure pile must be a sufficient distance from the barn so that it does not attract flies into the stable. For horse owners who enjoy having the family horse at home and don't mind the work involved in caring for him, the backyard stable is an ideal arrangement.

The Commercial Stable

For horse owners without the space, time, or inclination to care for their horses at home, there is another solution: the commercial boarding and riding stable. Some stables provide only a stall, and the owners take responsibility for the care of the animal. This is called rough board. Other stables provide a total-care service, requiring nothing from the owner except payment. This is called full board.

Although it may cost more money to board a horse in a stable, there are several advantages to doing so. Many stables have an enclosed riding arena that can be used day or night, all year round. Such stables will generally have better facilities and more equipment than the home stable and may offer instructors and trainers to work with horses and riders. In addition boarders and their horses can organize and participate in a number of activities, from trail rides to horse shows.

Commercial stables are generally busy places. Here is what a typical day at a boarding stable might be like:

Before most people even think about going to work in the morning, stable employees are on the job. The first task of the day is to check the horses and make certain that they have all had a safe night. Then the horses are fed grain, watered, and hayed. After breakfast the first of many cleanups begins. Stalls are mucked and new bedding is put down. Next the horses are turned out for their daily exercise. In larger stables there is generally limited "turnout" space, and so horses go out in shifts. While the horses are outside, the stable workers get a chance to tidy up the barn: to clear hay from the aisles, take inventory of feed and hay supplies, put away any sheets, blankets, and wraps from the previous night, and prepare for the remainder of the day's activities.

This large commercial stable offers both boarding and riding facilities for privately owned horses.

Stalls are mucked while horses are turned out to pasture for exercise.

As the horses return from turnout, they are groomed and prepared for the day's exercising or training. After grooming they are tacked up and taken to the exercise ring. A sound, healthy horse that is fit and exercised regularly may only need a brief workout at the walk, trot, and canter each day. However, a horse in training (or one preparing for a full season of shows and competition) will be rigorously worked for perhaps an hour or more.

Following the workout session the horse is cooled down slowly, groomed, and returned to its stall for a rest. The horse's tack is cleaned and returned to the tack room. Soon it's time for midday hay and perhaps a visit from the blacksmith, veterinarian, or dentist. Horses in commercial barns see the blacksmith, the veterinarian, and the dentist on a regular basis. During the afternoon stalls are cleaned and water buckets filled.

As the day draws to a close the horses are fed grain and once again given hay. A final check is made at the end of the day and, if necessary, the horses are blanketed. Then it's lights out for the night until the following morning, when the whole process begins again.

A day in the life of a well-cared-for horse is busy and filled with many different people: muckers, grooms, riders, trainers, blacksmiths, veterinarians, and barn managers. Each person fills an important role in keeping horses healthy and happy.

Patricia Erwin, BARN MANAGER

Patricia Erwin is barn manager at Old Salem Farm in North Salem, New York.

"Old Salem Farm stables forty-five horses. I am directly responsible for their care and well-being, even though I don't do 'hands-on' tasks such as grooming and training. It's my job to supervise and coordinate the daily schedules for each of the horses. I also manage a staff of ten grooms.

"My day usually begins around six thirty in the morning and ends at about seven in the evening. I work six days a week and have my days off on Monday when the barn is closed.

"I got interested in horses when I was very young. I was kind of a 'barn brat,' always hanging around horses. By high school I had become a pretty good rider and was able to teach the beginners. I received a small cash commission from the lessons I taught. From there I went on to other barns, working and teaching. I also got my Associates degree in Animal Center Management and became a certified veterinary technician. I learned a lot about the medical aspects of animal care, and this is still very useful to me.

"After school I went to Brazil for three years and taught English riding. I worked on a farm that stabled twenty horses and became their barn manager. Sometimes it was pretty hard, because the Brazilian men weren't used to having a woman or an American as their boss—and I was both! When I returned to the United States, I worked for a veterinarian. We took care of horses at breeding farms and the racetrack. I gained a lot of experience in each of my jobs, and all of it helped me to become the barn manager at Old Salem.

"One of the things I really like about my job is that I'm always busy. I order all the feed, hay, and supplies that we use at the barn. Our horses can consume four to five tons of hay in a month—we go through a lot! I make sure that the veterinarian comes when she's needed, and I set up her regular visits. I supervise the shoeing schedule of each horse so that he sees the blacksmith at regular intervals or when something goes wrong, like losing a shoe. I also make sure that the owners know what is going on with their horses. Even though I don't groom or train, I need to be able to tell the owners exactly what their horse has been doing or how his training is going. Most barn managers also handle all the recordkeeping, but here it's handled by someone else, who has it computerized.

"I used to think that someday I would have my own barn. It was always my dream. Since I've had this job, that's changed. I guess I've realized how hard it is to handle everything that can (and does!) go wrong. I realize that I'm lucky to do this as a job. I still get to do what I love, and yet I'm not the farm owner.

"Now I have another fantasy. I'd like to live in Europe for a few years—in someplace like Germany—and manage a farm to support myself while I learn from the European trainers. The Europeans have a riding heritage, a real tradition, and in many ways their riding is more advanced than ours."

The Groom

Next to his owner, a horse probably knows his groom best. Their relation goes far beyond a shiny coat and a nicely braided mane. Grooms are responsible not only for keeping horses clean and neat in appearance but also for keeping tack in good condition, assisting the horse (and rider) before and after daily workouts, and helping in shipping and competition. Most grooms are also in close touch with the horse's overall mental and physical condition because they oversee a horse's activities throughout the day. The groom is liable to spot health, soundness, and behavioral problems early on because of this close contact.

Items for the Grooming Box

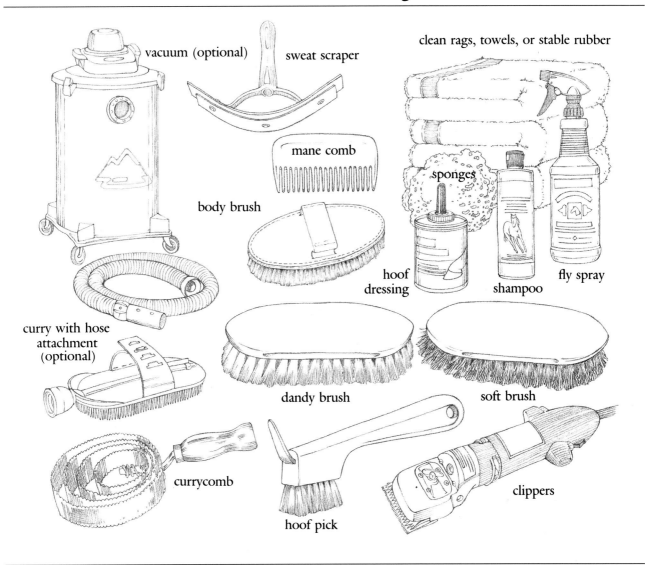

vacuum (optional)

sweat scraper

clean rags, towels, or stable rubber

mane comb

sponges

body brush

hoof dressing

shampoo

fly spray

curry with hose attachment (optional)

dandy brush

soft brush

currycomb

hoof pick

clippers

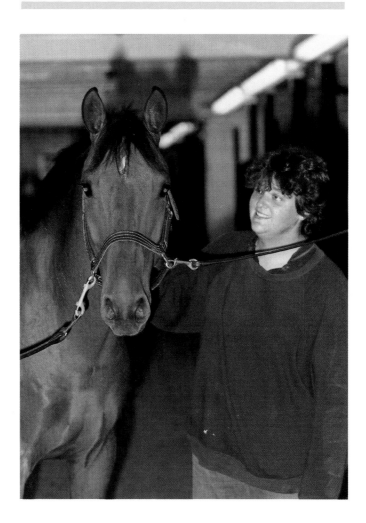

Betsy Shanahan, GROOM

Betsy Shanahan is a groom at Old Salem Farm in North Salem, New York.
She is one of 10 grooms who care for the 45 horses boarded at the farm.

"My job is to take the best-possible care of the horses. I work six days a week, from about six thirty in the morning to six at night. On show days I'm here even later, often until eight. I have Mondays off because the barn is closed.

"Grooming involves overseeing the actual care of the whole horse—and there is a lot more to it than just brushing them. Each groom here has four or five horses to take care of. When I come to work in the morning, I check over all my horses and see that they are well and happy. After I feed them, my work really begins. I make sure that they are turned out wearing the proper protection—that might mean bell boots or a warm winter blanket. Then I scrub out the horse's feed and water buckets and make sure he has plenty of water to drink when he comes back inside. I muck out the stall and put in clean, fresh bedding for when the horse returns. Occasionally, when the walls get really dirty, I wash the stall down with bleach and a degreaser. I really care that everything gets done right!

"I groom the horses twice a day: once right before they are tacked up to be ridden, and again right after. During the summer the horses can get so sweaty from working that grooming can involve lots of baths. Most of the larger barns, like ours, have vacuums with special attachments for a horse's coat. So after I've currycombed the horse to get the dirt out of his skin and hair, I vacuum him to make sure all the dirt is really gone—not just brushed back into his coat.

"I'm also responsible for taking care of all the horse's clothes and equipment. I make sure that his blankets stay clean (and in one piece!) and that any special devices needed (like a cribbing strap or a hay rack) are properly used. I care for the owner's tack and tack up the horse before it is ridden.

"When the horse is ill, or lame, or has any physical problem, I'm usually the one to carry out the veterinarian's instructions. The horse may need to be poulticed several times a day or wrapped. Hosing, soaking, hand-walking—I do them all.

"In addition to taking care of the horse, I get involved in exercising when the owner is away or the horse needs some extra attention. For instance, I might longe the horse if he were recovering from an injury and not able to work yet.

"A good groom has a lot to do with how well a horse performs. And hopefully, you and your horses get to be good friends."

Jerry Trapani, FARRIER

Jerry Trapani has been a farrier for more than 20 years.

"Shoeing horses is a very rewarding profession. The satisfaction of watching your equine 'clients' moving well, winning in competition, or traveling soundly again after a lameness makes worthwhile the demands of this difficult job.

"Being a farrier means more than nailing on horseshoes. It means working with veterinarians, breeders, and trainers to learn about the individual needs of each horse or foal, and involves making emergency calls and working long days in all weather conditions. Farriery is not a nine-to-five job!

"It takes considerable training to become a proficient farrier. To get an idea of what the career demands of you, try to spend some time with a farrier, going with him on his rounds. The best way to learn is through the old apprenticeship system. There are also many good farrier schools, which offer various programs. A complete listing is available from the American Farriers' Association, P.O. Box 695, Albuquerque, New Mexico 87103."

The Veterinarian

The horse doctor will be another regular visitor to the well-cared-for horse. Like the blacksmith, he or she makes barn calls with a fully equipped truck, stocked with medicines (some even have running water!), instead of a little black bag. A horse is liable to meet his vet soon after he is born. He will receive regular vaccinations and deworming preparations from his vet over the years. The veterinarian performs gelding operations on colts and does prepurchase examinations. He or she also treats accidents and disease, and may perform euthanasia on horses who are suffering and cannot be helped.

When a horse is too sick to be treated in the barn, the vet may recommend that it be moved to a local clinic or hospital or to an equine hospital affiliated with a veterinary college.

An operating room in an equine medical clinic. Horses are brought to surgery on a trolley or a sling and placed on an operating table, which can be raised or lowered by a hydraulic lift.

James A. Fischer, D.V.M.

Dr. Fischer's veterinary practice includes small animals as well as horses.

"I became a veterinarian because of my love of animals, an interest in biology and medicine, and my wish to work outdoors and with horses. To become a vet takes a minimum of four years of college undergraduate studies and four more of veterinary school. Then you take state and national board exams (I'm licensed in New York State and Connecticut). I worked with a veterinary group as an assistant to gain as much experience as I could, because equine medicine is a very specialized field.

"One of the things I like most about my work is the social aspect—meeting people. I also like diagnostics and internal medicine—the challenge of finding out what's wrong and correcting it. What I like least are the hours. I often put in ten- or twelve-hour days, every day, with no day off for a month. It doesn't give me a lot of time to spend with my family.

"Young horse owners should know their horses well so that they are able to tell when they are sick. If you think your horse has a problem, be sure to contact your veterinarian.

"For those who aspire to become veterinarians, a love of animals is a prerequisite. You should also have an aptitude for science, particularly biology, and a good scholastic grade average.

"Veterinary schools look for a high grade average during the college years and a well-rounded individual who has experience with animals. It's important to communicate well and have an outgoing personality. Some veterinarians are not successful in practice because they don't deal well with people."

First-Aid Kit for the Barn

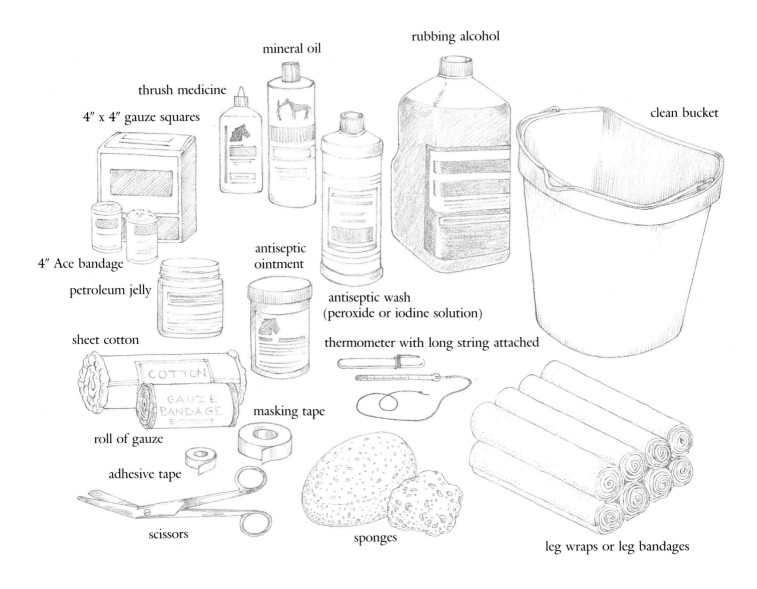

thrush medicine

mineral oil

rubbing alcohol

clean bucket

4″ x 4″ gauze squares

4″ Ace bandage

petroleum jelly

antiseptic
ointment

antiseptic wash
(peroxide or iodine solution)

sheet cotton

thermometer with long string attached

roll of gauze

masking tape

adhesive tape

scissors

sponges

leg wraps or leg bandages

Stable Vices

Horses' bad habits are easier to prevent than they are to cure. Here is a list of some of the more common vices that horses develop as a result of boredom, anxiety, or stress:

Cribbing (chewing): The horse chews wood, buckets, blankets, or anything else within reach and may gulp large quantities of air at the same time. Cribbing leads to loss of condition and is dangerous for horses that are prone to colic.

Windsucking: The horse grasps onto the door of its stall or a fence or bucket and pulls back while gulping air. This is different from cribbing, and some horses do both.

Biting: The horse bites anything in its stall, horses in adjoining stalls, or its handlers.

Weaving: The horse stands in one spot and swings its head back and forth while shifting its weight from one front hoof to the other.

Tail and head rubbing: Much like weaving, although this can also be caused by parasites or skin fungus.

Stall kicking: The horse kicks at the stall walls when bored or waiting for food.

Stall walking: The horse endlessly paces the stall, usually wearing a track in the bedding along the perimeter of the stall.

Pawing: The horse paws repeatedly at the floor, wearing down shoes and occasionally doing damage to the hoof and leg.

A horse with no bad habits should never be kept near a horse with vices, as they often mimic each other.

A horse in the act of cribbing and windsucking.

Many stables have a radio playing and keep "pets" for the horses, to amuse them: dogs and cats are common horse companions.

VI

TACKING UP

Tack

Tack is the equipment a horse wears. It can be plain or fancy, modestly priced or expensive. The incredible assortment of equine equipment available in saddlery shops reflects the many styles of riding and various types of work that horses perform.

Halters

The halter is the single most common item worn by the domestic horse. The halter allows the horse to be led and tied. It should be sturdily constructed and well fitted. Halters are usually made of leather or nylon, with brass buckles and hardware.

Lead Lines

A lead line snaps onto the fastener ring of the halter for leading, grazing, or tying. Sometimes called a lead shank, it can be made of leather, nylon, or cotton rope.

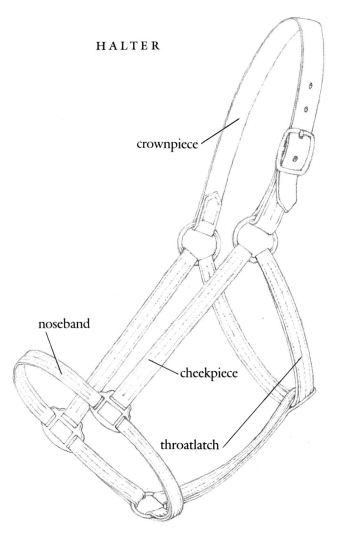

HALTER

crownpiece

noseband

cheekpiece

throatlatch

Bits and Bridles

A bit is a metal (stainless steel or copper), rubber, or plastic piece held in the mouth of the horse by the bridle. The bit and bridle work together as a unit and are controlled by the rider through the use of the reins. The bridle holds the bit in the horse's mouth and, through the reins, transmits the commands of the rider to the horse. Depending on their design, the bit and bridle work by exerting pressure on several sensitive spots of the horse's head and mouth. These spots are often called pressure points.

Most bits function by encouraging the horse to move away from the pressure (or pain) caused by the action of the bit. In order for the bit to affect the horse's performance in a positive way, it must fit the horse properly. A bit that is too large may slide right out of the horse's mouth, and a bit that is too small will pinch its lips. The mouthpiece of most bits measures between 4½ and 5½ inches. The bit must also be appropriate for the work the horse is to perform and for the skill of the rider. A severe bit in the hands of an inexperienced rider has been compared to a razor in the hands of a monkey. The bit and bridle are two of the three most important pieces of tack used by riders (the other being the saddle). Few other pieces of tack permit such direct contact between horse and rider.

PRESSURE POINTS

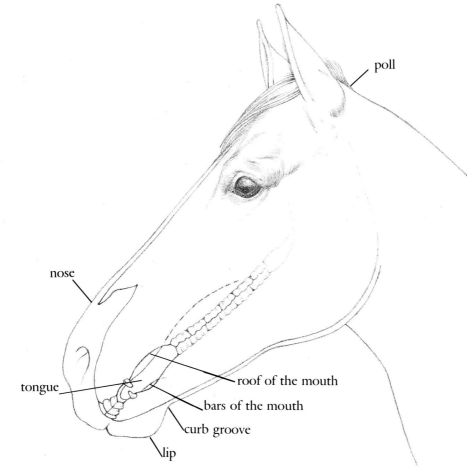

poll

nose

tongue

roof of the mouth

bars of the mouth

curb groove

lip

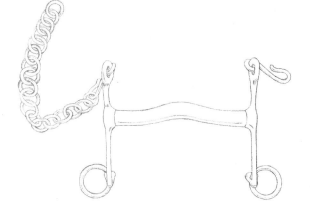

The curb bit consists of a straight or arched metal mouthpiece connected to parallel sidepieces. The cheekpieces of the bridle attach to the top rings of the curb bit. Hooks on the upper rings of the bit can hold a curb chain, which rests against the curb groove of the horse's lower jaw. The curb reins fit through the lower rings of the bit. When the curb bit is used simultaneously with a snaffle bit (bridoon), it then becomes part of a double bridle.

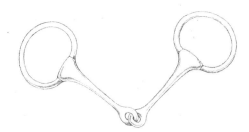

The snaffle bit is commonly used by both English and Western riders. Basically a snaffle is two metal rings connected by a metal or plastic mouthpiece. The mouthpiece is jointed and may be thick or thin, twisted or smooth, and have differing shapes and sizes of rings.

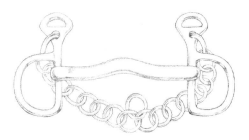

The Kimberwick Pelham uses a single set of reins.

The gag bit and bridle look something like the snaffle bit and bridle but differ greatly from it. The cheekpieces of the gag bridle pass through small holes in the bit rings and then attach to rings that are fastened to the reins. The bit is then made to rise and fall by pressure from the reins.

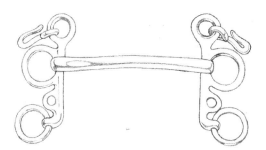

The Pelham bit is similar to the curb but combines the effect of the snaffle and curb into one bit. It is used with two sets of reins and a curb chain.

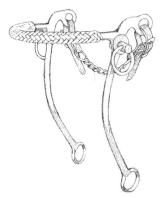

The hackamore bit is technically not a bit at all, because no portion of it rests inside the horse's mouth. Rather, it puts pressure on the horse with a noseband, which reduces or cuts off the horse's air.

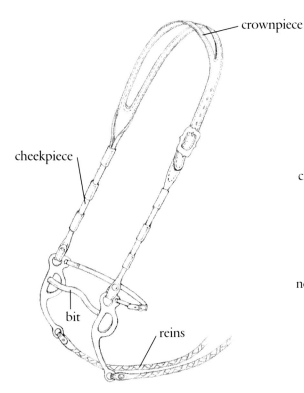

crownpiece

cheekpiece

bit

reins

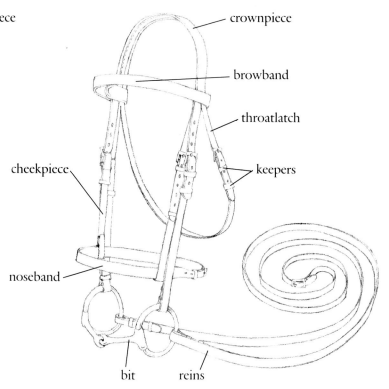

crownpiece

browband

throatlatch

keepers

cheekpiece

noseband

bit   reins

Some Western bridles are fitted with a sliding earpiece to be worn over one or the other ear or with a split-ear crownpiece that both ears fit between. Many Western pleasure riders use a bridle that resembles the English hunt bridle without the noseband.

Reins

When a rider uses the bit and bridle as a means of communicating with his horse, the reins serve as an extension of his hands. Reins are most commonly made of leather and can be laced, braided, rolled, or flat. They are also available in cotton web, linen cord, and rubber. The average English rein is five feet long and joined by a buckle. Western-style reins may be open or closed. They often have an extra piece of leather attached to the closed rein, called a romal, which acts as a crop or bat.

WESTERN-STYLE REINS

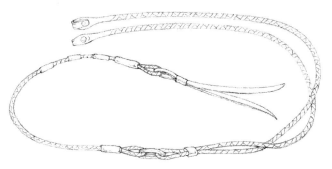

LACED ENGLISH REINS

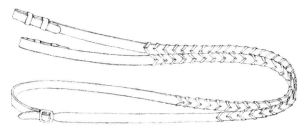

Martingales

The martingale is a restraining device that prevents the horse from tossing its head up (perhaps into its rider's face). The two commonest types of martingale are the running and the standing martingale.

The running martingale branches into two pieces ending in rings, through which each of the reins must pass. The running martingale puts pressure on the bit; the standing martingale attaches to, and exerts pressure on, the noseband. Both types of martingale attach to the girth.

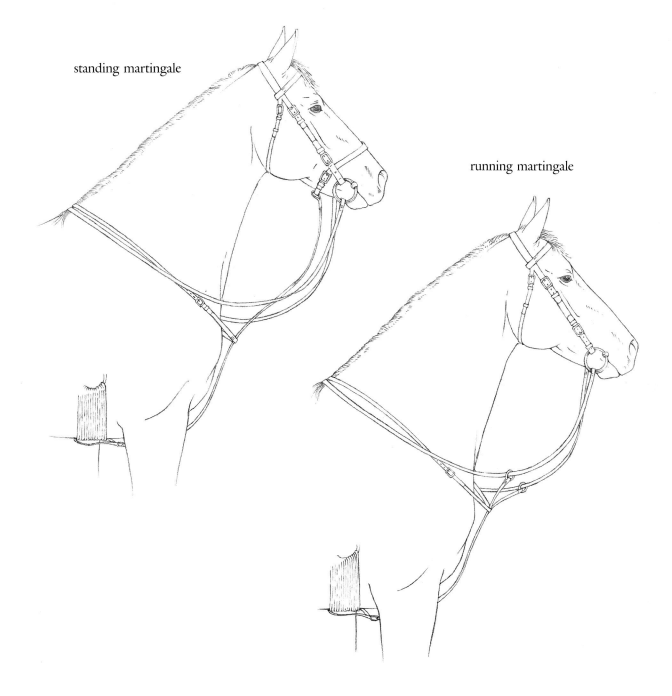

standing martingale

running martingale

Saddles

Although there are many different kinds of saddles, they all share two purposes: to protect the horse's back and to enable the rider to maintain his position. Every saddle is built on a basic structure called the "tree," which may be made from wood, metal, or fiberglass. The tree must be high enough to clear the horse's withers, strong enough to withstand pressure, and wide enough to rest properly across the horse's back. The tree is then padded, and the outer covering of the saddle (usually leather) is added. Saddles must be well made, properly fitted to both horse and rider, and well maintained. A good saddle can last a lifetime.

PARTS OF THE ENGLISH SADDLE

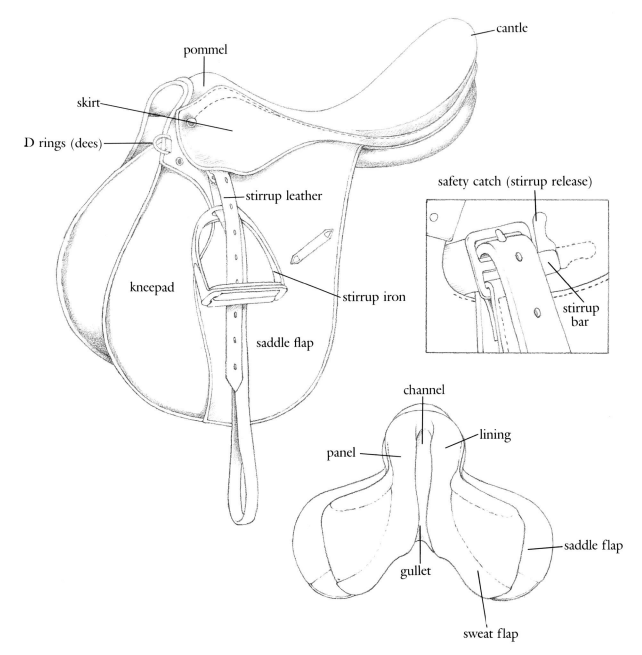

pommel

cantle

skirt

D rings (dees)

stirrup leather

safety catch (stirrup release)

stirrup bar

kneepad

stirrup iron

saddle flap

channel

lining

panel

saddle flap

gullet

sweat flap

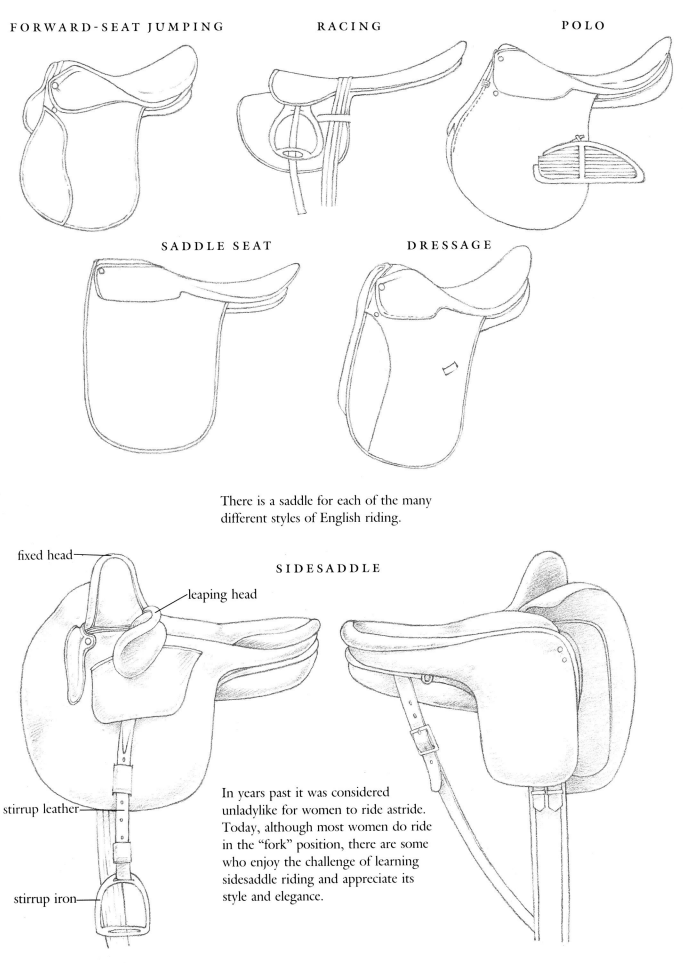

FORWARD-SEAT JUMPING

RACING

POLO

SADDLE SEAT

DRESSAGE

There is a saddle for each of the many different styles of English riding.

SIDESADDLE

fixed head

leaping head

stirrup leather

stirrup iron

In years past it was considered unladylike for women to ride astride. Today, although most women do ride in the "fork" position, there are some who enjoy the challenge of learning sidesaddle riding and appreciate its style and elegance.

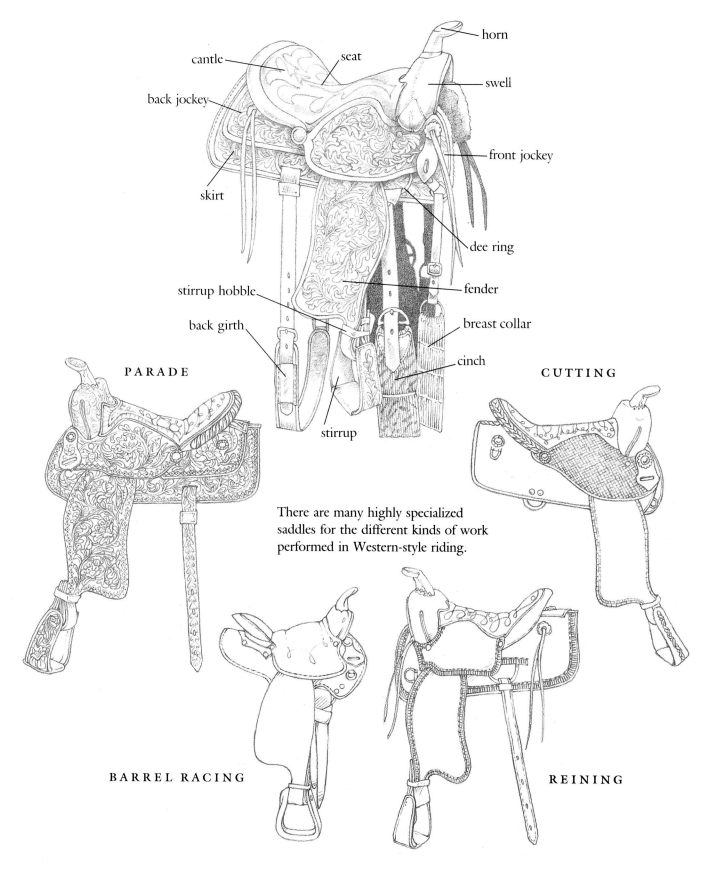

horn

cantle

seat

swell

back jockey

front jockey

skirt

dee ring

fender

stirrup hobble

back girth

breast collar

cinch

stirrup

PARADE

CUTTING

There are many highly specialized saddles for the different kinds of work performed in Western-style riding.

BARREL RACING

REINING

Saddle Pads

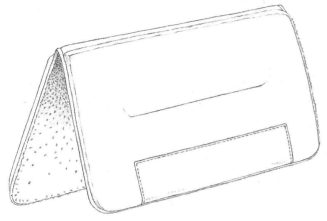

Both English and Western riders use saddle pads—made of foam rubber, washable fleece, or quilted cotton—for protection, absorbency, and additional support. Many come with a loop that fits around a billet, anchoring the pad in place.

BAREBACK PAD

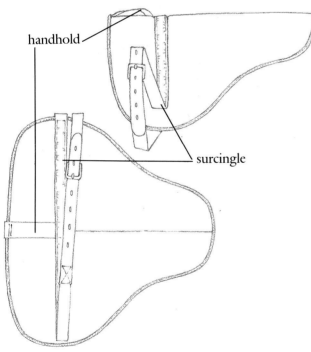

handhold

surcingle

Bareback riding offers closer contact with the horse than any other form of riding. Special canvas saddles protect the rider from the horse's sweat.

Girths

The girth holds the saddle in place. It attaches to the saddle's billets, which in most saddles are connected to the tree. The use of one girth over another is determined by the type of saddle and personal preference. Girths are available in leather, cord, linen, mohair wool, cotton, nylon, polyester, and web. Fleece girth covers are available to prevent chafing.

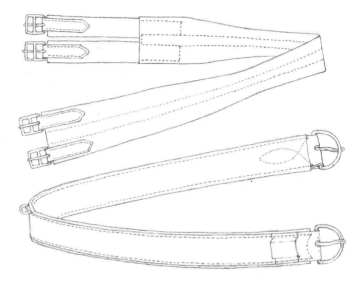

Stirrup Leathers and Stirrup Irons

Stirrup leathers, often simply called leathers, are long strips of leather that attach the stirrup irons to the saddle. The leather loops through the stirrup iron and onto the stirrup bar under the saddle flap and can be adjusted. Most leathers have prepunched holes and a buckle so that they can be shortened or lengthened according to the rider's needs.

Stirrups, sometimes called irons, hold the rider's feet in place. Those for English riders are made of a nonrusting metal, such as stainless steel or nickel-plated steel. Jockeys prefer a lightweight, roundish iron sometimes called a racing iron. Some stirrups are offset: the opening for the stirrup leather is set to one side, so that the stirrup is tilted. This allows for better leg and heel position. Some stirrups are designed strictly for safety and have a rubber band connecting all three sides. In the event of a fall the rubber band releases, preventing the rider from being dragged. Many stirrups come with various types of treads, allowing the rider to get a better grip with his boot.

The Western stirrup leather is called a fender and is made of flat, smooth leather that prevents chafing of the rider's leg. Unlike English stirrups, Western stirrups are made of wood and covered with leather. Stirrup hoods are often used to protect the rider's feet and keep them warm.

Boots, Wraps, and Bandages

Horses are subject to injury, especially leg injury, because of the way they are built and the athletic life they lead. Because of the fragile nature of the horse's legs and the importance of keeping them protected and in top condition, there is a wide array of boots, wraps, and bandages available.

Ankle boots are padded to work as shock absorbers.

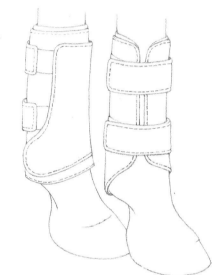

All-purpose boots provide protection during workouts.

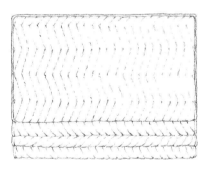

Quilted leg wraps provide support under bandages.

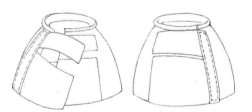

Bell boots protect a horse whose hind feet scrape against his front feet while working.

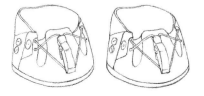

An easyboot is a protective device used to cover an injured or unshod hoof.

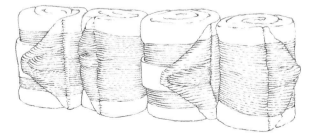

Polo bandages offer flexible support and protection.

· 80 ·

Fashion and Function: Horse Clothes

When a horseman talks about sheets and blankets, he isn't talking about bed linens. He's talking about his horse's clothing! Unlike most other animals, a well-cared-for horse is liable to have more than a few items of clothing.

New Zealand rug: A traditional, regulation-wear, standard blanket for horses, it offers protection from water, cold, sharp objects—and even other horses! Made of tightly woven, waterproof canvas with leather trim, this is the blanket that is suitable for anything a horse can think of to do to it.

Winter blanket: For horses lacking heavy winter coats or in harsh climates, winter blankets can be used alone or with a New Zealand over them.

Cooler: An essential for any horse that lives in all but the warmest climates. After a hard workout a horse needs time to cool down and warmth in which to do it. A cooler is often put on until the horse's body temperature has returned to normal and the horse is dry. Use of a cooler prevents the horse from getting a chill.

Cotton duck sheet: This basic item provides warmth without bulk in moderately cool areas.

Sweat sheet: These cotton sheets help to keep racehorses and other competition horses free of chills and cold after working.

Fly sheet: This simple mesh sheet can reduce the torment many horses endure from flies and other biting insects.

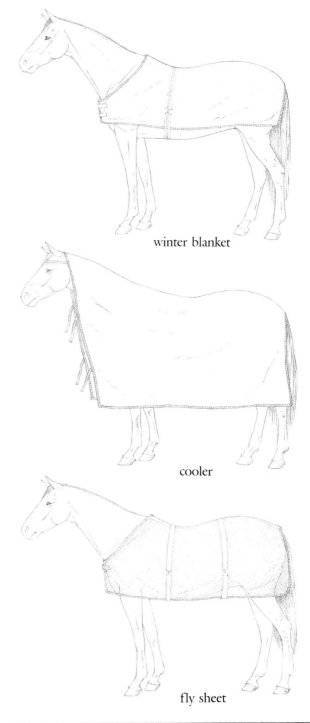

winter blanket

cooler

fly sheet

Two horses enjoying a brisk fall day in their sheets.

VII

TRAINING AND RIDING

Training

Horses are trained so that they can safely and obediently carry a rider and respond to the rider's wishes on command. Without training, horses and humans would have little they could do together. Even the most basic training should improve the horse's balance and self-carriage under the weight of a rider.

On the Longe

A young horse's first formal training often begins with a longe line (pronounced "lunge"). This is a webbed rein or line, approximately 25 feet (7.6 meters) long, which is fastened to the horse's halter or bridle. The trainer holds the line while the horse moves around him in a circle. At first the trainer may lead the young horse around in the circle until he will continue

on his own, but once he does, the trainer uses the longe whip to keep the horse moving forward, as shown on page 82. The whip is *never* used in a way that will frighten, hurt, or confuse the horse—it is used to convey the same messages that the rider's leg will later transmit. The horse is gradually introduced to wearing a bridle with a bit and to carrying the weight of a saddle. By the time mounted training begins, the horse is well accustomed to feeling these pieces of tack.

Under Saddle

When mounted training begins, the horse must learn to accept the rider's weight and movements of the rider's legs and hands. These are all aids (signals) that help tell the horse what the rider wants him to do.

A young horse under saddle is taught to

respond to the aids for the walk, trot, canter, halt, and back. He is encouraged to move briskly forward at all gaits and given simple exercises—walking in a straight line, trotting in a circle or a serpentine—to develop balance and concentration. This is all part of his training on the flat.

As training progresses, the horse will be given suppling exercises. These exercises strengthen him and make him more athletic, just as the exercises human athletes do prepare them for different kinds of competition. The horse will be ridden in patterns known as *schooling figures,* such as figure eights, circles, and half circles, which are designed to improve his physique and keep him mentally alert. The schooling figures are a lot like those used by figure skaters in their compulsory exercises, before they go on to the more artistic freestyle skating competition.

Schooling (practicing) in the ring is often offset by quiet trail rides to keep the horse from becoming bored.

Basic training prepares the horse for many purposes. He may stop at this level of training to be strictly a pleasure mount, or he may go on to become a "specialist" and receive additional training in a specific area.

Training on the Flat

Despite the differences in the kinds of work that horses may be asked to perform, they all begin with the same basic training. Known as training on the flat, or *dressage* (French for "training"), it is important for all horses. Dressage teaches obedience; improves balance, suppleness, and flexibility; and enhances athletic ability. It is the work that prepares horses for all further training—including that which may lead to advanced levels of dressage competition, where horses perform difficult movements in prescribed sequences.

Training on the flat prepares horses that will be ridden Western style for many of the movements they will learn to execute later on: spins, rollbacks, flying lead changes, and sliding stops. It also gets them ready to work around other animals, such as cattle.

Saddle horses (gaited horses) develop their artificial paces early in their training. Various devices (some of them controversial) assist the trainers in creating the high-stepping gaits particular to their breeds.

Training over Fences

If a horse is going to be a jumper or hunter, his specialized training will usually start with *cavalletti,* or ground poles. Trotting over evenly spaced cavalletti helps teach the horse to pick up his feet, to develop the rhythm and timing necessary for jumping, and to pay attention to what lies ahead. A valuable preparation for jumping, it benefits both horse and rider.

Once the horse has established a steady rhythm, a low crossrail is placed at the end of the row of cavalletti. This will be the horse's first real jump. Other crossrails can be added at even distances as the horse progresses, so that eventually he will be jumping smoothly and confidently over several crossrails in sequence.

Before a horse is asked to jump the complex courses of advanced jumping competitions, he will be schooled over gymnastic jumps to develop his confidence and skills. Gymnastic jumping exercises allow the horse (and rider) to vary the jumping situations in order to develop timing, stride, form, and judgment.

A young horse and junior rider working over a ground pole and low crossrail. The ground pole will help the rider to adjust her horse's stride so that he meets the takeoff spot correctly. This is sometimes called "seeing the distance."

Riding Lessons

Riding cannot be learned through a quick series of lessons or by reading a book, although a book may help a student to understand what he is being taught in his lessons. Learning to ride is an ongoing process—every ride gives the rider more experience. Good riding requires instruction, practice, and many hours on many different horses.

The First Lesson

A beginner should start on a quiet, experienced horse with smooth gaits. First the beginning rider learns to mount from the left (near) side of the horse. Stirrups are adjusted to the proper length, and then the new rider takes up the reins. He or she will then be shown how to adopt and maintain the correct position in the saddle. After the rider assumes the proper leg and hand positions, the horse is asked to walk on. The first several lessons are sometimes conducted on the longe line, held by the instructor, who guides the horse as the beginning rider learns to sit properly and gets used to the movement of the horse. During the first lessons the rider is usually working at the walk and the trot. It takes time to develop a "feel" for the rhythm of the horse's strides, and to master the technique of sitting or rising (posting) to the trot.

When beginners feel comfortable with the basics of riding (the walk, trot, canter, halt, and back), they can then decide what other kinds of riding to learn. Like horses, riders may eventually become specialists in jumping, cross-country riding, dressage, equitation (hunter seat, saddle seat, and stock seat), or pleasure horse competition (Western or English).

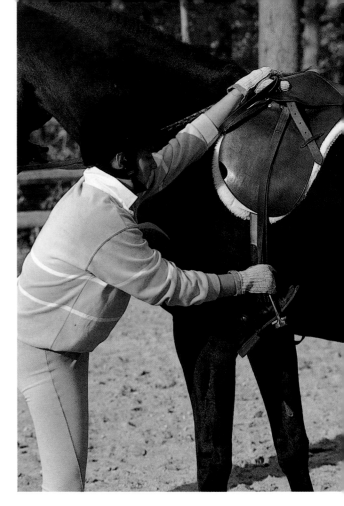

Learning to mount unassisted.

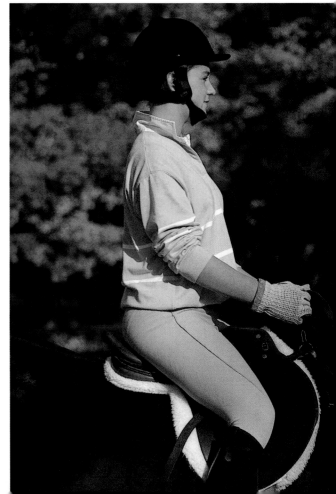

The proper position in the saddle.

Mounted training begins with
exercises to develop balance and a
familiarity with the horse's
movements.

In later lessons the rider takes up the
reins and masters each of the gaits.

George Morris, TRAINER, JUDGE, INTERNATIONAL RIDER

At age 14, George Morris was the youngest person ever to win both the Maclay and the Medal equitation championships. Mr. Morris now judges, teaches, and competes internationally.

"Historically, hunter-seat equitation has been the basis for all American riding, whether it is combined training, dressage, or riding hunters and jumpers.

"Unfortunately, equitation today has become an end unto itself. I see it becoming stylized, and artificiality creeping in. To overcome this, when I judge I try to shake the riders up by getting them away from the mechanics and testing their natural talents and understanding of the basics. When they get to world-class competition, that's what they'll need. In one equitation class I asked the riders to change horses—and to change their own saddles—in the middle of the ring. You'd be surprised how difficult that was for some of them!

"Competing in equitation requires so much hard work, time, and dedication that it almost becomes a career. But mastering the rudiments of equitation should enable a rider to fox hunt, ride show hunters, train green horses, and be an all-around horseman.

"What I brought with me from my equitation days was a good foundation and technique. I went through the junior ranks with the late Gordon Wright [a prominent American trainer for several decades], so I had a good background that included position, schooling exercises on the flat, a lot of experience jumping different horses, fox hunting, and showing open jumpers. It was a wonderful foundation for Bert de Némethy [coach of the United States Equestrian Team at that time] to take over.

"Our U.S.E.T. riders have benefited from training over low jumps that simulate courses of higher jumps. They don't have this [the equitation division] in other countries. Equitation is like eighth grade, the junior-amateur division is high school, and grand prix work is college."

The Spanish Riding School of Vienna

The Spanish Riding School of Vienna was founded in the late 16th century to teach the art of horsemanship at its highest level. The school took its name from the Spanish horses that were the ancestors of the Lipizzaners.

One of the most thrilling sights in the world of horses is to see the white Lipizzaner stallions going through their paces, with their riders dressed in reddish-brown coats and white breeches, high black boots, and hats. Like a troupe of ballerinas, they "dance" through the performance to classical music, executing the movements of high-level dressage correctly, but with grace and precision as well. At the Spanish Riding School horsemanship is elevated from a sport to an art form.

The horses that perform such miraculous movements as the "airs above the ground" were originally bred in the town of Lipizza near the Adriatic Sea, but today they are bred at the Austrian stud farm at Piber.

The horses have a beautiful and elegant setting in which to perform their exhibitions. Completed in 1735, the riding hall is decorated with white marble and crystal chandeliers. At each performance riders pause to salute a portrait of Emperor Charles VI, who founded the school.

Young riders at the school get their initial experience on older, well-trained stallions. They begin by riding on the longe line without reins or stirrups until they have developed deep, secure seats in the saddle. The senior *Bereiter*es, or riding masters, train the young stallions.

The white Lipizzaner stallions are the pride of Austria and are considered national treasures. Visitors to Vienna are always eager to buy tickets to a performance, and many tours of the city include a stop to watch the morning practice sessions.

The splendid riding hall of the
Spanish Riding School in Vienna,
built in 1735 by Emperor Charles VI
of Austria.

A Program at the Spanish
Riding School of Vienna

Young stallions. The young Lipizzaners have dark coats, which turn white as they mature. They are ridden in schooling figures, which prepare them for future training.

1. **Steps and movements of the classical school.** The horses perform many exercises that are required in Olympic dressage tests as they go through their routine.

2. **Pas de deux.** Two horses perform as mirror images of each other and in step with the music, like dancing partners.

3. **Work on the short rein and between the pillars.** These exercises prepare the stallions for the "airs above the ground." The *piaffe* and *passage* are done between two pillars in the center of the arena or with a trainer standing beside the horse, holding him with a short rein.

4. **Work on the long rein.** Well-trained horses, controlled with long reins and a whip, execute the steps and movements of the classical school.

5. **"Airs above the ground."** These are done both in hand and under saddle (without and with a rider on the horse's back) and include the following:

    Levade: The horse squats deep on its haunches, with its forefeet off the ground, and holds this position for several seconds, resembling a living statue;

    Courbette: The horse performs several forward leaps on its strong hind legs without its forefeet touching the ground;

    Capriole: The horse leaps into the air and, at the height of the jump, kicks out with its hind legs.

6. **School quadrille.** This ballet of the white stallions has four or more performing in precise unison to music.

These beautifully trained Lipizzaners are performing some of their specialties.

Work on the long reins.

The capriole on long reins.

Performing the quadrille.

Anne Gribbons, TRAINER

Anne Gribbons has served on various committees of the U.S. Dressage Federation (U.S.D.F.) and the American Trakehner Association. She competes, trains, and judges at all levels of dressage competition. *

"Enthusiasm for the education and promotion of junior and young riders was slow to develop in the dressage community until only a few years ago. To me this was very surprising, since the obvious place to look for new talent and future victories is among our youngsters. Through the Competitors' Council of the United States Dressage Federation, we tried for several years to get support for more competitions and challenges for the under-twenty-one set, but the reception was cool. Thanks to the efforts of Captain Andrew de

Szinay [a prominent figure in American dressage] in conjunction with the U.S.D.F. executive board and regional representatives, things are looking up.

"About five years ago I was told by a prominent competitor that 'dressage is not a kiddie sport.' I could not agree less. Although this discipline requires above-average maturity and a certain amount of perseverance, my experience has been that if you introduce youngsters to classical riding early, most of them find it fascinating.

"Training the junior or young rider is extremely rewarding. What the youngsters lack in experience they make up for in enthusiasm, suppleness, and receptiveness. Most have no fears or feelings of embarrassment, and usually their power of concentration is remarkably good.

"I have been lucky to be able to follow some of my students from bouncing eight-year-olds in training level to fairly sophisticated Fédération Equestre Internationale riders in the early teens. Probably all instructors who work with children hope to see some of them become trainers, teachers, judges, and perhaps even team riders one day."

---

*According to U.S.D.F. rules, a junior in dressage is a competitor who has not reached his 18th birthday by December 1 of the previous year. A young rider is a competitor who has reached his 15th birthday but not his 21st by December 1 of the previous year.

Raul de León, TRAINER

Raul de León is a former Cuban national jumping champion who has been teaching in the United States for many years, most recently at Westmoreland Davis Equestrian Institute in Leesburg, Virginia.

"Young riders learn the most from good teachers. In learning to ride, there is an important triangle: horse, instructor, and student.

"A well-trained horse is the best teacher. For the beginner, the school horse should be quiet and docile and have gaits that are fairly comfortable. If he has a smooth canter, it helps the student master this gait at an early stage in his riding. Good basic training is important for the horse because the less refined his schooling is, the less he is able to teach.

"The riding instructor, ideally, should enjoy working with people. He should have good communication skills and be even-tempered. It also helps if he is an avid student himself, because it keeps him from becoming stale in his teaching and from losing his enthusiasm.

"In addition to being a good rider, the teacher must have common sense. He can't become involved with competing vicariously through his students to the extent that he harms their development or forgets about safety. He must have enough authority to be able to say 'no' to a student or parent with respect to buying a horse or going to a show.

"The student must be sincere in his desire to learn, trust his teacher (they must be compatible), and have enough self-discipline to get the most out of his lessons. You get out of the lessons only what you put in. The student should be able to accept criticism and authority.

"I have worked with many young people. At Westmoreland Davis, where I teach, there are mostly young adults, age eighteen and up. But interest is more important than age. I feel that a child should not begin serious instruction until he has become a certain physical size; eleven or twelve is usually a good age. Small children may be allowed to ride a quiet horse or pony on the lead line and should be encouraged to watch horse shows and lessons.

"I like teaching as much as I like riding. I have both a love for the art of teaching and for horses, and I have combined the two in my life. That's why my position at Westmoreland Davis is so right for me—I'm doing what I love to do."

Captain Andrew B. de Szinay, TRAINER AND JUDGE

When he came to the United States in 1950, the late "Captain Andy" brought with him a wealth of knowledge and experience acquired in the cavalry in his native Hungary. He served on numerous national committees and was a guiding force behind the Young Rider Dressage Program in this country.

"Growing up in Hungary, I rode from the time I was eight or nine years old. I loved it, and when I got older, I decided to apply for the cavalry. I started my officer's career as a second lieutenant with the Second Royal Hussars.

"During the fall and winter training period we rose at six A.M. and rode from seven thirty until nine thirty. Then we moved on to the stables to care for the horses and tack until lunchtime, which was between twelve and one. From one to five, we practiced tactical exercises on foot. This was our schedule on Monday, Tuesday, Wednesday, and Friday. The Hussars were expected to be in the barracks by nine P.M.—occasionally they could stay out until eleven or twelve or take a weekend off.

"Thursday was cavalry 'rest' day, when the horses underwent a rigorous health inspection. The troops rode on Saturday morning and had the rest of the weekend off. Within this general time schedule, the officers had to find time to work with their own horses.

"By late spring we were ready for more complex training. A full day or several days were spent on exercises with our mounts that simulated wartime conditions. Furloughs started on June 29, St. Peter and Paul's Day, when the grain was traditionally ready for harvest (the Hussars were furloughed in two groups). In August we had 'general exercises' away from the barracks for several weeks. Then in September we prepared for another new year of training.

"The advanced riding course for cavalry officers was based on dressage. Riding equaled schooling equaled dressage. The 'seat' was a dressage seat. Jumping came later. The advanced course lasted nine months, six days a week, and was a great learning experience, with riding, riding, and more riding! It was one of the best times of my life.

"As a cavalry instructor I taught Hussars eighteen to twenty years old, about the ages of young riders competing in the United States today. Some of the Hussars had almost no experience with horses, and we had a year in which to turn them into good riders and cavalrymen. Of course, I can't treat young riders in the United States like Hussars or I'd be deported! The conditions aren't the same. What we do today is 'spot' training through clinics and periodic instruction. We don't have the continuity that existed in the cavalry and which is the proper foundation for riding.

"The cavalries reached their peak just before World War I, when they became the elite troops of each army. Then mechanization appeared, and the cavalries gradually disbanded. Today's equestrian life sorely misses the centrally trained, uniformly instructed teachers provided by the cavalry. I hope a solution will be found in the United States—the sooner, the better!"

dressage   fox hunter   jockey

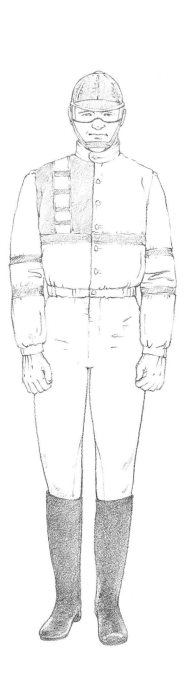

Dressage riders wear a top hat, black or dark blue shadbelly (tailcoat), canary vest, white shirt with white stock, white breeches, white gloves, and black dress boots with spurs. Dress is identical for both men and women.

The formally attired male fox hunter wears either a top hat or black hunt cap, a scarlet ("pink") coat, white shirt with white stock, canary vest, tan or white breeches, white string gloves, and black dress boots. Women wear black or navy coats and black hunt caps.

The jockey's costume is lightweight and colorful. It consists of racing boots (often brown-topped), white jockey pants, and racing colors ("silks")—the custom-made jacket that shows the stable colors. The jockey's helmet has a leather harness and is covered in colors that match the jacket.

eventer   show jumper   western

 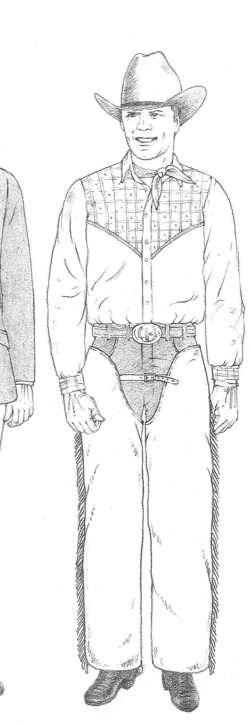

The cross-country phase of three-day eventing calls for the most casual and practical of riding clothes: black or brown dress or field boots, breeches, a turtleneck, rugby or polo shirt, and string or rubber-palmed gloves. The eventer's helmet has a mandatory chin strap and is covered to match the shirt.

Formal show jumpers wear a black hard hat with optional harness, solid dark coat, and black dress boots. Women wear a white shirt with choker or stock, white breeches, and black dress boots, while men wear a white shirt with white tie, white breeches, and black boots with brown tops.

"Workmanlike" best describes the look of the Western show rider. Standard items include the Western-style brimmed hat, snap-front long-sleeved shirt with collar, jeans or trousers with chaps, and Western-style riding boots. Some common accessories are a coordinating vest, trophy belt with large buckle, neckerchief or bolo tie.

VIII

HORSES AND PONIES AT WORK

Yesterday's workhorse is largely a nostalgic memory in the modern world. For the most part, today's horses "work" on sports fields and in leisure-time pursuits. But there are still some jobs in which horses haven't been replaced by machines, and some places in the modern world where things continue to be done as they were a century ago.

Kinds of Workhorses

Farm Horses

The sight of a draft horse hitched to a plow is rare in highly mechanized countries. However, in some rural and remote areas it is still possible to find draft horses demonstrating the strength, stamina, and willingness necessary for agricultural work.

"Horsepower" comes in many breeds, from

During Vermont's sugaring season, this team of Belgian drafts helps collect sap from the trees.

Ranch Horses

The rancher depends on horses for many things. If he owns a large ranch, he may have to cover many miles at a time when he inspects his land, fences, and herds. On a working ranch horses are used to cut cattle (separate one or more from the herd) and for roping.

Some ranches are *dude* ranches, which serve as vacation places for guests (the term "dude" is a Western expression for an Easterner or tourist). Horses on a dude ranch often double as school or trail horses, teaching visitors to ride and carrying them on daily excursions or pack trips.

The best horses for this purpose are usually crossbreeds (a mixture of Quarter Horse, Appaloosa, and Pinto, for example), about 15 hands, and eight to 18 years of age. Geldings are preferred over mares, because they are less likely to be temperamental; one of the most important qualities in a ranch horse is a good disposition. On a typical dude ranch the horses carry wranglers (cowboys) and dudes on daily rides through valleys, over mountain trails, and across rivers from spring to fall. Then the horses are given the winter off. They are taken to a winter pasture that offers plenty of good grazing. In early spring the horses are rounded up, which may take several days or weeks, and brought back to the ranch. Then, before guests are allowed to ride them, they are ridden a few times by the wranglers because some of them are reluctant to get back to work!

Ranchers still use horses to drive cattle from one place to another.

Horses are brought back to the ranch
after months in their winter pasture.

Packhorses

What is a pack trip without a good packhorse? These dependable animals carry big loads over mountains and across terrain that an automobile cannot travel. They make it possible for riders to spend many days and nights along the trail in comfort.

Packhorses (mules or burros may also be used) carry tents, clothing, and cooking utensils. Their loads are distributed across their backs in such a way that the weight is even, leaving their hindquarters unhampered. They follow one behind the other, a rope attaching them from the halter to the rigging of the horse ahead, all of them led by a rider on horseback.

A good packhorse is strong, surefooted, and well-mannered. He is able to pick his way carefully over the narrowest ledge and rockiest path while carrying heavy loads. He may not be as exciting as other horses one encounters in equestrian sports, but he is indispensable to all who enjoy lengthy riding trips and camping out.

Although this packhorse carries a heavy load, his heavily muscled shoulders and hindquarters are unencumbered.

Packhorses must be even-tempered
and get along well with other horses,
as they spend a great deal of time
following one another closely up and
down rocky trails.

The A.S.P.C.A. and the Horse

In 1863 an American by the name of Henry Bergh was working as secretary of the American Legation in St. Petersburg, Russia. One day Mr. Bergh came upon the driver of a Russian carriage who was giving his horse a vicious beating. When Bergh tried to stop him, the man said angrily, "It's my horse—I can do as I wish with it!"

Mr. Bergh began to think about the rights of helpless animals. When he returned to New York City, where horses were the main source of transportation, he waged a one-man battle against cruelty to animals. Often ridiculed, he was labeled "the great meddler." But with time he was able to enlist support, and by 1866 his actions led to the establishment of the nation's first anticruelty law and the foundation of the American Society for the Prevention of Cruelty to Animals.

Although the A.S.P.C.A. is now associated primarily with the concerns of dogs and cats, it was begun in an era when horses were used, and often abused, in everyday life. During World War I, when horses were heavily used by the military, the A.S.P.C.A. staff lectured at forts and barracks on proper horse care in times of warfare. The role of the A.S.P.C.A. underwent gradual changes as horses were replaced by motor vehicles on city streets and in the armed forces.

In 1929 the first A.S.P.C.A. "Good Hands" horsemanship class was held at New York's National Horse Show. Eleven young women under age 15 competed and were judged on "hands and seat." Horsemanship over fences was introduced in 1933 with the first Maclay class—known then simply as the Horsemanship Cup, which is presented by the A.S.P.C.A. and

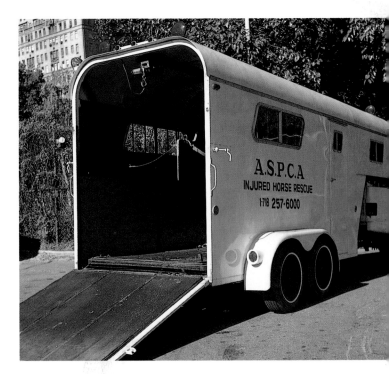

The A.S.P.C.A. horse ambulance in New York City.

was donated by Alfred B. Maclay, Esquire. Although today the Maclay has become one of the most prestigious horsemanship events in the country, the A.S.P.C.A. has not forgotten its educational origins. Each junior who competes is sent, along with a membership card, a booklet on horse care with a suggested reading list.*

Today humane agency officers routinely check to see that the horses who pull carriages through New York City's Central Park are properly cared for. Carriage horses are now taken off the streets when temperatures climb to over 90 degrees Fahrenheit (32 degrees Celsius). The A.S.P.C.A. provides a horse ambulance when it is needed and a water truck for the hot summer weather in Central Park.

*For information on the A.S.P.C.A. and the Maclay class write to: The American Society for the Prevention of Cruelty to Animals, 441 East 92nd Street, New York, NY 10128.

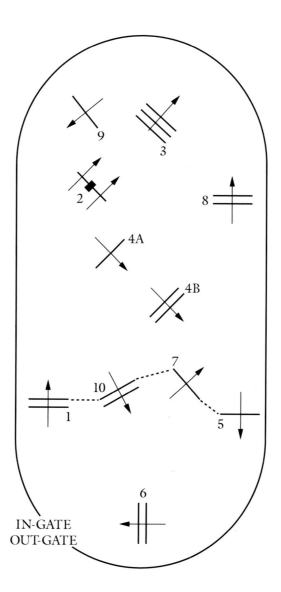

IN-GATE
OUT-GATE

This course was used in the 1987
Medal Finals and was designed by
Linda Allen, Susan Pinckney, and
Stephen O. Hawkins.

IX

HORSES IN COMPETITION

Although there are many sports involving animals, equine sports are unique in that horse and rider compete as a *team*. This mysterious and wonderful partnership between human and animal is one of the most appealing aspects of competitive horse sports.

Horses and riders compete for many reasons. Some riders like the challenge. Others use competition as a "measuring stick" to compare their horses to those of other people in the same divisions. For some, competing successfully is proof that their horse's training is going well. Breeders and stables derive favorable publicity from their horses' victories in competition.

Most countries have federations to govern riding activities and set forth rules and guidelines for equestrian competition. In the United States the American Horse Shows Association (A.H.S.A.) has this function. The list of divisions in the *A.H.S.A. Rule Book* (see box on page 128) illustrates how diverse the world of horse shows can be. International competition is governed by the Fédération Equestre Internationale (F.E.I.).

Horse Racing

"They're off!" shouts the announcer, and the starting gate snaps open to release its equine

The track bugler announces the post parade to the public.

dynamos, thundering hooves carrying them around the track at more than 40 miles per hour (64 kilometers per hour).

Horse racing is popular because it is exciting to watch and to bet on winners. Although there are different kinds of racing, including Quarter Horse racing, harness racing, steeplechasing, and point-to-point racing (see page 125), Thoroughbred racing attracts the most attention, offers the largest purses (cash winnings), and has the most universal appeal.

Flat Racing

Racing on the flat (over a track with no obstacles) originated in England during the 17th century with the English Thoroughbred, a horse built for speed. The British colonists brought the sport to the New World, where horses raced on short dirt tracks improvised in the wilderness. By the late 1800s the sport was popular, but very disorganized. It was time for an organization to lay down rules that governed the tracks and races and to regulate what had, in fact, become an industry; thus the American Jockey Club was formed in 1894. Its responsibilities include keeping the Thoroughbred stud book, registering horses, and maintaining records that keep track of all important racing business in the United States.

Without the racehorse, there is no race. For this reason training really starts with the breeder. Once the breeder finds a buyer, the horse is on his way. The new horse owner then makes what is probably the most important decision affecting the life of his horse—he chooses a trainer. The trainer takes over the total care of the young racehorse, bringing together a team of horsemen, including veterinarians, blacksmiths, grooms, exercise riders, and jockeys, who prepare the young racehorse for his work and

continue working with him throughout his career.

Before a colt or filly feels the weight of a saddle or rider on its back, it is "ponied" (led by a rider on an older, more experienced horse) for a while. Bit by bit the young horse is introduced to new experiences. Soon it is taken on quiet gallops in the company of several other horses, where, hopefully, a new feeling is aroused in the young horse. This feeling—the instinct to run, to race, and to win—has been inbred over many, many generations.

The earliest a Thoroughbred can race is at the age of two. As the horse matures, he progresses to races that further test his speed and stamina. The racing season also matures through the year, providing longer distances as the season progresses. This culminates in racing's biggest events—the Triple Crown races (the Kentucky Derby, the Preakness Stakes, and the Belmont Stakes) and the Breeders' Cup.

Jockeys, or professional racehorse riders, usually weigh less than 110 pounds (about 50 kilograms) but are extremely strong. Because they ride with short stirrups, they communicate largely with their hands, their whips, and their voices. The jockey's success depends on his ability to bring out the best in his horse. The horse may have the speed, but the jockey shows him how to use it to win a race.

Any newcomer to racing should understand the concept of "handicapping," a means of making horses of varying experience and ability more equal in competition. Handicapping refers to how much weight is carried by the horse. The less weight a horse carries, the less interference there is with his speed. Therefore a horse is handicapped when he is required to carry extra weight; this evens the chances between older, more experienced, and more successful horses and younger, less seasoned ones.

At *handicap* races the racing secretary is given

Breeding, training, and the ability of
the jockey all play a part in determining
which horse will win. But it is often
the Thoroughbred "heart" that tips the
balance and propels one horse over
the finish line a split second before the
rest of the field.

the job of assigning weights; in *allowance* races the horse's previous winnings determine weight allotments; and in *weight-for-age* races the horse's age and sex, the track's distance, and time of year are used for figuring the weight it will carry. *Stakes* races such as the Triple Crown races are for horses of the same age carrying the same weights—and they are not handicapped.

In *claiming races,* which account for the majority of horse races in America, the horses are classified by their value and are for sale. Such races are a way for trainers and professional horsemen to watch horses perform on the track, spot talent, and, if they are lucky, acquire it. A claiming race works in the following way. All horses are entered according to their approximate value. Thus an owner who feels that his horse is worth $5,000 would enter it in a $5,000 claiming race. (This keeps the field of competitors fairly equal and prevents good horses from competing against less talented ones.) Right before post time (the start of the race) sealed claim bids can be made on any horse in the upcoming race. The race takes place. After the race, if there is only one bidder for a particular horse, the bidder can claim the horse. If there are multiple bidders, a drawing takes place, and the winner of the drawing gets the horse. Of course if no claims are made, the owner goes home with the horse.

Jockeys wear racing silks in the colors of the stable whose horse they are riding. Even their helmets have colorful covers!

David Nuesch, JOCKEY

David Nuesch became a jockey at the age of 17.

"I was born into the horse business, so it was likely that I would wind up in one of the fields. I chose racing because it's probably the most intense of all.

"I get up at five A.M. and go out to the exercise track. I usually get on the horses pretty early, before it's even light. Sometimes I go to different barns to consult with trainers. Then I go to the racetrack. You have to be there by eleven if you're riding in the first race. I have lunch there—a sandwich, or something like that. I try to avoid junk food. I don't eat much candy. Then I ride all afternoon. I usually ride almost to the last race. I get home at about five thirty and eat dinner and watch my races on videotape, relax, or do whatever I have to do. I try to go to bed at nine. I like to get at least eight hours of sleep. That's about it—horses all day long!

"You always try to improve. Trainers notice both the good and the bad, but the mistakes—they notice those first! You remember those and you try to correct them. That's why I like to watch the races again at night. If you know something happened in one part of the race, you can watch it carefully.

"Riding keeps me in condition—I don't do any other exercise. I'm five feet two inches tall and weigh 100 pounds.

"I have determination, and a lot of people have noticed that I'm very relaxed on a horse.

"Try to start riding as young as you can. It takes a long time to learn. The best place is at a farm. I was born on a farm, and I learned from the greatest person around—my father. He owns Braeburn Training Center in Crozet, Virginia. We've had people who came from jockey schools, where they have five-week courses. Nobody who ever learned how to ride well enough to make a name for himself learned to ride in five weeks! My father always says, 'It takes two years to make a bad rider.' It supposedly takes ten before you're a good rider. It's one of the hardest sports to learn. You have to know the horse. With any other sport, you just have to know the rules, but here you're dealing with another animal, another brain. It can work against you, and you have to try to make it work *with* you.

"Kids who are in a hurry later realize how little they really know. My father says he's still learning every day."

The famous racehorse Secretariat, with
jockey Ron Turcotte up and handler
Eddie Sweat, just before the running
of the 105th Belmont Stakes. (He won!)

Steeplechasing

Steeplechasing, or racing over jumps, originated in England and Ireland as an outgrowth of fox hunting and officially became a sport in the early 1800s. There are three kinds of steeplechase races. *Hurdle* races, the simplest, are generally used as a proving ground for younger horses that are just beginning their careers in the sport. In these races the pace is most important, and speeds often exceed 30 miles per hour (48 kilometers per hour). *Brush* racing rules specify the number and type of obstacles in each race: 12 fences in the first two miles (3.2 kilometers), six in each succeeding mile (1.6 kilometer), one ditch, and one water jump. The most famous brush race in steeplechasing is the Grand National, held annually in England. *Point-to-point* races, over obstacles resembling those on the hunt field, are for entrants who qualify by having hunted with a recognized pack. They are also referred to as *timber* races, because they include post and rail fences.

Steeplechasing has long been recognized as one of the more dangerous horse sports. So much so that even the most famous of all, Great Britain's Grand National at Aintree, is coming under close scrutiny.

Harness Racing

Racing horses in this sport are driven, not ridden, on the flat. In harness races the driver (called the reinsman) sits in a two-wheeled vehicle (called a sulky) and guides his horse around a track at the pace or the trot. The Standardbred horse dominates the harness racing scene—both at the pace and the trot.

These Standardbred horses, pulling "sulkies," or lightweight carts, are racing at the pace.

It's a race to the finish with the famous Affirmed in the lead!

Polo

The game of polo originated in Persia in the Middle Ages, was brought to England early in the 19th century, and came to the United States in the 1880s. An exciting, risky, and visually spectacular game, it has now attained world-wide popularity.

Polo is played on a grassy field 300 yards (274 meters) long with goalposts at either end. For the mounted players the object is to score as many goals as possible by hitting the ball through the opposing team's goalposts, using a long-handled mallet.

The game is usually divided into four to six time periods called "chukkers" of seven and a half minutes each. After the bell the players continue until the ball is out of play or the umpire stops the game. There are three minutes between chukkers and a five-minute break at halftime. Each time a goal is scored, the players change sides—that way, in case the wind is blowing from one direction, it evens up their chances. The umpire watches for fouls and keeps the riders' behavior safe for one another and the horses. (Penalties are imposed by giving the other team a free hit.) To keep the competition as fair as possible, players are rated and handicapped. These ratings are regulated by the United States Polo Association.

Horses used in the game are referred to as polo ponies, but they are actually small horses, usually between 15 and 15.3 hands. In general they are agile, strong, and even-tempered. Polo ponies are more than just a ride to the players—good players recognize the contribution of the talents of the horse, often crediting him by saying that "the polo pony is 75 percent of the game." Ponies are commonly used for about two chukkers per game, with a rest period in between. For that reason polo players need several horses, called a "string" of polo ponies.

The best polo ponies are thought to be bred in Argentina, where Thoroughbreds are crossed with Criollos, small but resilient Argentine riding horses. Polo ponies must be robust in mind as well as body.

Polo is an expensive sport, but more people than ever are finding a way to play—in fact, many learn it while learning to ride. Its popularity is growing very quickly at the collegiate level, where play culminates each year in a national tournament. In polo, as in most other equestrian sports, men and women compete on an equal basis.

Dressage

Translated most simply, dressage means "training." Yet for those who have witnessed the performance of a horse executing advanced-level dressage movements, it seems an understatement to simply describe that horse as "trained." The high-level dressage horse is *transformed*. Beauty, grace, elegance, lightness, and precision are the by-products of years of systematic and progressive training of both horse and rider. So dressage can be either basic training for any other equestrian activity or a total commitment to the discipline itself.

In dressage competitions the horse and rider perform a programmed test in an arena 198 feet (60 meters) by 66 feet (20 meters) wide.

A smaller arena of 132 feet (40 meters) by 66 feet (20 meters) may be used for training level. Letters placed around the arena serve as guidelines for the execution of the required movements.

The tests start with the basics of training level, which are fairly simple, and progress in difficulty through levels 1, 2, 3, and 4 of the American Horse Shows Association tests. After that the horse and rider enter the F.E.I. (Fédération Equestre Internationale) levels of dressage, which include tests known as the Prix St. Georges, Intermediaire I and II, and the Grand Prix. The Grand Prix is the highest level, in which the horse is required to perform the piaffe and passage as well as changes of the canter lead at every stride. These are called

---

1987 AHSA Tests
(All trot work is sitting unless otherwise specified.)

TRAINING LEVEL, TEST I
Approx. 4 min. (sm.), 5 min. (std.); 180 possible points.

1	A	Enter working trot rising
	X	Halt, salute; proceed working trot rising
2	C	Track to the right
	B	Circle right 20m
	B	Working trot sitting
3	Between	
	F & A	Working canter, right lead
4	E	Circle right 20m
	Between	
	E & H	Working trot rising
5	CMEK	Working walk
6	K	Working trot rising
	B	Circle left 20m
	B	Working trot sitting
7	Between	
	M & C	Working canter, left lead
8	E	Circle left 20m
	Between	
	E & K	Working trot rising
9	A	Down center line
	X	Halt, salute

Leave arena at free walk on long rein at A.

TRAINING LEVEL, TEST 2
Approx. 3½ min. (sm. arena), 4½ min. (std.); 170 possible points.

1	A	Enter working trot rising
	X	Halt, salute; proceed working trot rising
2	C	Track to the left
	A	Circle left 20m
	B	Working trot sitting
3	Between	
	M & C	Working canter, left lead
4	C	Circle left 20m
	E	Working trot sitting
5	A	Working walk
	F-E	Free walk on long rein
	E	Working walk
6	H	Working trot rising
	C	Circle right 20m
	B	Working trot sitting
7	Between	
	F & A	Working canter, right lead
8	A	Circle right 20m
	E	Working trot rising
9	MXK	Change rein
10	A	Down center line
	X	Halt, salute

Leave arena at free walk on long rein at A.

"flying changes," and although they appear as light and easy as skipping, they are actually very difficult to do. It takes a very talented horse and rider to reach this level.

Dressage is scored on a basis of zero to 10. The judge gives each movement in the test a score: zero means the movement was not performed, and 10 is perfect. Both are very rare—most scores fall somewhere in the middle. The scores on the test paper are added up by the scorekeeper and changed into percentages, and the horse with the highest score is the winner. In dressage competitions only the horse's execution of the movements is scored—not the ability of the rider.

In 1973 the United States Dressage Federation (U.S.D.F.) was formed to promote interest in dressage in the United States through programs, awards, educational events, and information. In recent years a Junior/Young Rider program was begun for riders up to the age of 21. According to U.S.D.F. spokespeople, the best way for young riders to get started in dressage is to join one of the many regional organizations throughout the country devoted to the sport.

Dressage is one of the Olympic equestrian sports. Although it is not as popular with spectators as the more exciting jumping events, at its highest level it is as beautiful to watch as a ballet.

Dressage freestyle competition, called the *Kür*, requires riders to devise riding routines to the music of their choice. The *Kür* is comparable to freestyle figure skating and very artistic.

The musical freestyle may be performed at any of the levels of dressage competition. The judge looks for the movements required at that level and rates both the technical execution of those movements and the overall artistic impression of the presentation designed by the rider.

Belinda Baudin on the talented mare Alegría.

Gunnar Ostergaard, the noted dressage trainer and competitor, on Elektron.

Robert Dover, DRESSAGE RIDER

Robert Dover, a leading international competitor in dressage, rode for the U.S.E.T. in both the 1984 and 1988 Olympics.

"I've been involved with dressage since I was thirteen. I started my riding career in a dressage barn—Trakehnen Farm in Toronto. Then I moved to the Bahamas and joined Pony Club. Elizabeth Lewis, a dressage rider, was my first teacher, and through her I met the late Colonel Bengt Ljungquist of Sweden and studied with him.

"I've always been a self-disciplined kind of person. I like to have every little detail perfect. Although I was an "A" Pony Clubber and did some eventing, I always had a special love of dressage.

"There are a few individuals who gravitate toward dressage at an early age, although, of course, it's healthy to do a lot of things in riding. With a special child you can begin to work in dressage right away. With others you have to feel them out to see if they have the right discipline and concentration for it."

Robert Dover on his 1984 Olympic mount, Romantico, performing a half pass to the right.

Show Jumping

Jumping began as a sport in the 18th century, with origins in both European cavalry exercises and British fox hunting. It continued at horse fairs and agricultural fairs until international competition officially began in the early 1900s. At that time the sport was advanced by Italian cavalry officer Federico Caprilli's adoption and popularization of the "forward seat," the style of riding jumpers still use today. By 1912 show jumping was an Olympic sport. Today show jumping is one of the most appealing of all equestrian spectator sports. Because it is uncomplicated—the horse and rider must only jump a course of fences with the fewest faults (penalties) as quickly as possible—the spectator needs to know little about the diversities of the show world to appreciate it as an exciting and beautiful competition.

Although it may look simple, show jumping is demanding physically and mentally for both horse and rider. Riders and horses must *together* negotiate a course of varied obstacles—walls, spread fences, upright jumps, water jumps, and others—separated by distances that require just the right approach, calculated quickly but very accurately by the rider. Sometimes the fences are arranged in combinations—two or three obstacles to be taken as a series. Horses that go "clean" (jump without faults) often have to go on to a jump-off, with the fences raised and a clock recording their times. The horse with the least jumping faults and time faults, or the shortest time, is the winner.

Today jumping is an exacting and thrilling sport, requiring boldness and ability on the part of the horse and careful planning, focus, and sheer nerve on the part of the rider.

Megan Furth, a young West Coast rider, began Grand Prix jumping when she was 16.

Joe Fargis, OLYMPIC JUMPING COMPETITOR

Joe Fargis was a 1984 Olympic jumping gold medalist.

"It was a special moment [winning the gold medal at the 1984 Olympic Games]. But I realized it would end. Life is back to normal, and I enjoy it.

"Everything is improving in our sport. The courses get better all the time. We have better horses, riders, and course designers than ever before. Ten years ago we had to go to Europe to get experience. Now we can stay home.

"The 1984 Olympics did a great deal to promote show jumping as a spectator sport. I feel privileged to have played a role.

"When I went back to Petersburg, Virginia, where I was living in 1984 after the Olympics, everyone knew who I was. They wanted to know, 'When is the next jumping event?'

"The Olympics are now a happy memory. If it happened all the time, it wouldn't be so special."

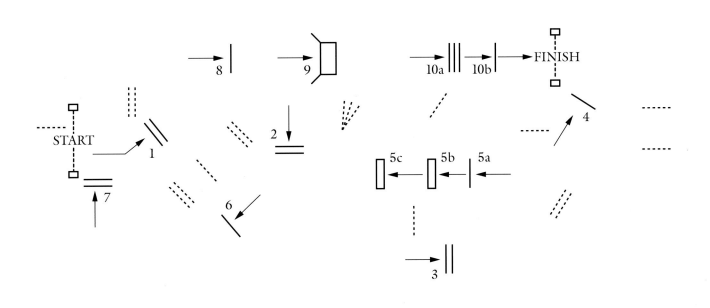

KEY

1	The Stable: Oxer	6	Helsinki Fence
2	The Olympic Fence: Oxer	7	Rain Forest Oxer
3	Beverly Hills Oxer	8	Windsor Castle
4	Sail Boat	9	Water Jump with White Gate
5a	Caracas Wall	10a	Redwood Triple Bar
5b	Oxer over Liverpool	10b	Redwood Vertical
5c	Oxer over Liverpool		

Joe Fargis rode the little mare Touch of Class around this course to win the gold medal in the 1984 Olympics.

Bertalan de Némethy, COURSE DESIGNER

Bertalan de Némethy, an expert course designer, also coached the United States Equestrian Team jumpers for 25 years. He was one of the most influential people in America in the sport of show jumping.

"The course designer has to consider many things—what materials he will be using, the footing, and the levels of the horses and riders who will be competing. The course should also be interesting to spectators. Course design is a little like decorating—it is an art.

"My ideas on course design are not based on how big or how wide the fences are, but on how the horse and rider perform together. The rider's judgment and communication with his horse and the horse's confidence in the rider should be so highly developed that they are in harmony. What separates the good from the not-so-good and the bad is not the size of the jumps but the combination of horse and rider. The best combination should win."

Combined Training: The Three-Day Event

Combined training, or three-day eventing, has been called the complete test of horse and rider because it consists of three disciplines: a dressage test on the first day, a grueling speed and endurance phase on the second day (including a steeplechase and cross-country course), and a stadium-jumping phase on the third day. Levels of difficulty progress from the training division through preliminary, intermediate, and advanced. Many competitions offer pretraining or novice divisions for those just starting out. The emphasis of the three-day event is on the second day—the F.E.I.'s ratio of importance for the three days is 3 to 12 to 1.

Combined training competitions can be held on a single day or over three days. Either event can be very challenging. The United States Combined Training Association (U.S.C.T.A.) promotes the sport and offers awards, much as the U.S.D.F. does for dressage.

Young event riders Molly Bliss (left) and Becca Lloyd (below).

Tad Coffin, EVENTER

Tad Coffin began riding as a Pony Clubber. In 1976 he was a double gold medalist at the Olympics, winning both the individual and the team gold medals for three-day eventing.

"As a young boy, I often dreamed of being a cavalry officer. How gallant and courageous those officers looked astride their prancing steeds as they paraded through the streets! How they seemed to be united as one being on the battlefield, an awesome force of courage, swiftness, and power! Stronger than this image was the sense of partnership between these officers and their chargers, the incredible bond between them created by so many shared experiences and so many hours spent together.

"The sport of combined training was developed as a test for officers and chargers, and as a teenager, it held great appeal for me. As a young rider, I was fortunate enough to be given a strong foundation in dressage and hunter seat equitation. I learned the skills that were necessary to develop a solid and enjoyable relationship with my horse. When I started combined training, the cross-country phase came easily to my horse and me. We worked together and in the sport found a way of expressing ourselves more fully than ever before. In addition to dressage and stadium jumping, we could gallop with the wind in our faces and soar over anything in our path. We spent much time together—hours on long rides through the country and in the stable after the day's riding was done.

"The sport of combined training gave me endless pleasure and an immense appreciation for the talent, character, and courage of my horse, for which I will always be grateful."

Australian eventer Barry Roycroft
tackling a very challenging water jump
at the 1988 Olympics in Seoul.

Combined Training

PHASES OF A THREE-DAY EVENT

Day 1: Dressage

Day 2: Speed and endurance

Phase A: Roads and tracks: a certain distance to be covered at a moderate trot

Phase B: Steeplechase (at 26 miles per hour, or 42 kilometers per hour) *

Phase C: More roads and tracks

Phase D: Cross-country (three to five miles, or five to eight kilometers)

Day 3: Veterinary inspection

Stadium jumping

A HORSE TRIAL

A horse trial is a scaled-down version of a three-day event and can take place over one to three days.

Phase 1: Dressage

Phase 2: Cross-country

Phase 3: Stadium jumping

* Distances, speeds, and height of fences vary depending on the level of competition.

Driving

Fast automobiles and four-lane highways may have replaced the horse and buggy of yesteryear, but there are still many people who enjoy a return to the past when they hitch up their horses or ponies for a pleasure drive or show.

Pleasure driving classes place emphasis on performance, manners, and the appearance of harness, vehicle, and attire. The entries compete at a walk, collected trot, working (medium) trot, and "trot on"—a faster, snappier trot. The horses are expected to stand quietly when asked, and the judges may have them execute a figure eight. *Reinsmanship* is primarily a test of the ability and appearance of the driver. He or she must be able to demonstrate all the gaits, rein back (back up), and perhaps do a figure eight or another test at the judge's request. There are also *obstacle* courses and *gambler's choice* classes in which the driver must negotiate obstacles, going around them without incurring penalties. In gambler's choice the more difficult parts of the course have higher point values. The driver tries to earn as many points as possible within a specified time period by choosing high-point obstacles.

Most shows offer classes for single horses or ponies and for pairs, but it is not unusual—especially in Europe—to see four-in-hand competition: four horses pulling one carriage. It takes a very skillful driver to get a smooth performance using a four-horse team!

Another exciting form of horse-and-carriage competition is *combined driving,* which is similar to combined training in that the entries perform a driven dressage test and then go on to drive cross-country and to negotiate a course of obstacles.

Driving classes are rapidly increasing in popularity in the United States. Some horse shows, such as the National Horse Show at New Jersey's Meadowlands, hold driving classes for fine harness horses such as Saddlebreds. There are also classes for Hackneys and for harness ponies and a roadster division, in which horses pull a wagon, buggy, or bike (two-wheeled vehicle).

Rita Trapani, WHIP (DRIVER)

Rita Trapani and her husband, farrier Jerry Trapani, collect and restore antique carriages. Rita has successfully competed in pleasure driving, reinsmanship, and obstacle-course competitions and belongs to the Paumonak Driving Club.

"The sport of driving is growing rapidly in this country. Twenty-five years ago, the Carriage Association of America was twenty-five people. Today there are approximately three thousand members. Since driving can be shared with friends and family, it's an ideal form of recreation. One good horse or pony can pull several people in a carriage or sleigh.

"I rode for many years before I took up driving. In driving, you remove yourself from the direct control you have when you're astride the horse. You polish your skills by working with your horse from a distance, connected to him by the shafts of the carriage and through the reins. Training comes through in the way you handle the reins and whip and the way your horse responds to voice commands. Training, skill, and trust are the three important elements.

"Driving is limiting in the sense that contact with the horse is indirect and because you need a lot of space—much more than just a riding ring. If you can't hack (ride) to a park or to competitions, you'll need a good truck and trailer to haul your horse, carriage, and harness.

"Caring for the vehicles and equipment is time consuming, but the pleasure and uniqueness of driving compensate for the work.

"Unlike riding, driving can be learned in a few weeks if you have access to a good horse, equipment, and instruction. It's important to have a horse or pony with a good disposition. You also need safe equipment and a knowledgeable teacher. If you have the aptitude and desire, you can go further and compete. Almost every driving competition has classes or divisions for junior whips, or drivers.

"Driving enables you to relive the past, when the family horse was part of everyday work and play. And it can be enjoyed year round—I've even restored an antique sleigh! A drive in the country brings you close to nature and is a most delightful way to spend your leisure hours."

Rita Trapani at the Devon Horse
Show with the Southside Club break,
designed by Jerry Trapani.

Rodeo and Western Competition

The rodeo is as much a part of the American West as wide-open spaces. First held in the early 1880s, rodeos have been called Frontier Days, Roundups, or even Stampedes. By this century towns throughout the West were organizing them; some grew into annual events of great popularity. And no wonder. Rodeos are colorful and exciting, and they feature many events—such as cutting contests and calf roping—that demonstrate the bravery and skill of cowboys and horses at work together.

The growth of rodeos led to the formation of the Rodeo Association of America in 1929 to establish rules, awards, and a points system—and eventually to the start in 1936 of an organization called the Cowboy Turtle Association, whose goal is to protect the interests of the contestants. The organization reputedly got its name when one of the founders said "Let's take it slow and easy" while they were deliberating.

Five events form the backbone of the modern Western rodeo. In *saddle bronc riding* a cowboy tries to ride a saddled, bucking horse for a minimum of eight seconds, using only an ordinary halter and a braided rope rein held in one hand. Top scores go to riders who use their spurs often and swing their legs high and often from front to back. Low scores go to riders who touch the saddle, rein, or horse with their free hand, lose a stirrup, or change the rein to the other hand.

Saddle bronc riders are judged on time—and style!

Eight seconds can seem like a long
time on a bucking bull!

Richie Fisher, TRAINER AND REINING JUDGE

Richie Fisher trains horses at his equestrian center on eastern Long Island. He serves as an adviser to the Long Island Horsemen's Society, a local club, and judges reining classes in Western shows.

"I started riding when I was about thirteen years old, at a barn in Brooklyn. I moved from Brooklyn to Long Island, and I've been there about twenty years now.

"I always did Western riding—barrel racing and reining. My specialty is breaking and training 'babies' and training horses for reining. Reining is my favorite event—I guess because it shows off the horse's responsiveness and all the ways it can maneuver. It's a sophisticated event as far as what you do with your horse and how your mind has to work. It's you and your horse together. I ride Quarter Horses for reining because they have a good mind and attitude, and very good balance.

"I also judge reining. To become a judge, you have to take a test. You are tested on how you judge a reining class, and every three years you must take a refresher test. As a judge, I look at the horse's attitude, to see if he is pleasant and happy in his work. I look at his way of going—does he move freely and naturally? I watch how he handles each maneuver, and whether he comes out of it quietly. I look at the overall pattern to see if it is appealing to me. There are seven or eight maneuvers in each reining pattern. I also notice how the rider handles the horse.

"I'm the only black reining-horse trainer and national reining judge that I know of. Not enough black people are exposed to riding. They don't know that they can do it. But they can."

Western Riding Pattern

This pattern tests Western riding abilities. Horses must perform at all gaits and be willing and flexible, following the requirements of the pattern.

WALK   - - - - - - - - - -

JOG   - - - - -

LOPE   ————

GATE   ≡

LOG   ▭

MARKER   X

BACK   ∿∿∿∿∿∿

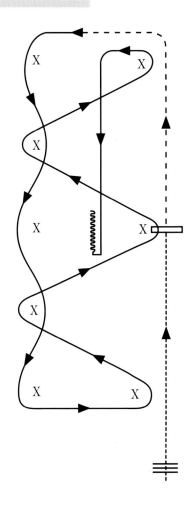

Silver medalist Greg Best and Gem
Twist tackle the Kwachon Gate at the
1988 Olympics in Seoul, South Korea.

The United States Equestrian Team

When an Olympic gold medal is placed around an athlete's neck and he hears the national anthem played, he and his fellow countrymen experience an enormous feeling of pride. It is a thrilling moment, but it doesn't happen overnight—it is the result of years of hard work and training.

Before World War II teams for international equestrian competition were provided by the cavalry. After the war, when the United States Cavalry disbanded, a new way had to be found to put together teams for international competition—namely, dressage, jumping, and three-day eventing. The answer lay in the creation of a civilian organization known as the United States Equestrian Team (U.S.E.T.).

By 1960 the U.S.E.T. had a home base at Gladstone, New Jersey. The team had good coaching from the beginning: Stefan von Visy of Hungary and Jack Le Goff of France coached the eventing riders, and former Hungarian cavalry officer Bertalan de Némethy coached the

The 1988 Olympic show-jumping team: Joe Fargis, Lisa Jacquin, Greg Best, and Anne Kursinski.

Anne Kursinski on Starman negotiating the Temple Jump at the 1988 Olympics.

Young riders across the country vie against each other in competitions sponsored by the United States Equestrian Team.

U.S.E.T. jumpers for 25 years.

The jumping team has enjoyed success in the Olympics, Pan-American games, Nations' Cup competitions, and many other international events. William Steinkraus rode Snowbound to win the individual gold medal at the 1968 Olympics in Mexico. In 1984 the United States won the team gold in jumping at the Los Angeles Olympics; Joe Fargis and Touch of Class won the individual gold medal and Conrad Homfeld and Abdullah won the silver. The U.S. team distinguished itself again at the 1988 Olympics in Seoul, South Korea, winning the silver medal; the winning combination of Greg Best and his mount Gem Twist earned the silver medal in individual competition.

The eventing team has also had many successes. In 1976 it won the gold medal at the Montreal Olympics, and young Tad Coffin (then 21) won the individual gold on Bally Cor. It was victorious again in 1984, winning the gold medal in Los Angeles.

There have been many talented U.S.E.T. riders in dressage, such as Hilda Gurney, Robert Dover, and John Winnett, to name just a few. In 1976 the American dressage team won the bronze medal at the Montreal Olympics.

Although the U.S.E.T. competes in the Pan-American games, international driving competition, and many shows and events throughout the world, success in the Olympics is one of its most important goals. Such successes are hard-won, and determined by many factors: footing, weather, course design, judging, and the condition of horses and riders, who may have traveled long distances to compete. Unlike many other Olympic events, equestrian competition involves the teamwork of two living beings, and both have to be in their best form on that particular day.

Phyllis Dawson rides Albany II on the
steeplechase course, part of the three-
day event at the 1988 Olympics.

U.S.E.T. Olympic Medals

PLACE, YEAR	EVENT	MEDALS	RIDERS
Stockholm, 1912 *	Three-day	Team bronze	
Paris, 1924 *	Three-day	Individual bronze	Maj. Sloan Doak
Los Angeles, 1932 *	Three-day	Team gold Individual silver	Lt. Earl Thomson
	Dressage	Team bronze Individual bronze	Capt. Hiram Tuttle
	Jumping	Individual silver	Maj. Harry Chamberlin
Berlin, 1936 *	Three-day	Individual silver	Capt. Earl Thomson
London, 1948 *	Three-day	Team gold Individual silver	Lt. Col. Frank Henry
	Dressage	Team silver	
Helsinki, 1952	Three-day	Team bronze	Charles Hough Walter Staley, Jr. John Wofford
	Jumping	Team bronze	Arthur McCashin Maj. John Russell William Steinkraus
Rome, 1960	Jumping	Team silver	Frank Chapot George Morris William Steinkraus
Tokyo, 1964	Three-day	Team silver	Lana duPont Kevin Freeman Michael Page J. Michael Plumb
Mexico, 1968	Three-day	Team silver	Kevin Freeman Michael Page J. Michael Plumb James Wofford
		Individual bronze	Michael Page
	Jumping	Individual gold	William Steinkraus

U.S.E.T. Olympic Medals (continued)

PLACE, YEAR	EVENT	MEDALS	RIDERS
Munich, 1972	Three-day	Team silver	Bruce Davidson Kevin Freeman J. Michael Plumb James Wofford
	Jumping	Team silver	Frank Chapot Kathy Kusner Neal Shapiro William Steinkraus
		Individual bronze	Neal Shapiro
Montreal, 1976	Three-day	Team gold	Edmund (Tad) Coffin Bruce Davidson J. Michael Plumb Mary Anne Tauskey
		Individual gold	Tad Coffin
		Individual silver	J. Michael Plumb
	Dressage	Team bronze	Hilda Gurney Edith Master Dorothy Morkis
Los Angeles, 1984	Three-day	Team gold	Karen Stives Torrance Fleischmann J. Michael Plumb Bruce Davidson
		Individual silver	Karen Stives
	Jumping	Team gold	Joe Fargis Conrad Homfeld Leslie Burr Melanie Smith
		Individual gold	Joe Fargis
		Individual silver	Conrad Homfeld
Seoul, 1988	Jumping	Team silver	Greg Best Lisa Jacquin Anne Kursinski Joe Fargis
		Individual silver	Greg Best

* From 1912 through 1948 the United States was represented at the Olympics by the U.S. Army Equestrian Team.

X

MORE HORSE ACTIVITIES

Pony Club

Pony Club began in England in 1929 as a means of preparing young children for the sport of hunting on horseback. Early Pony Club members were instructed in riding, the rules of the sport, and proper behavior for the hunt field. In 1953 United States Pony Clubs, Inc., was created. Today's Pony Clubs still emphasize the education of the rider, but now members learn about all phases of riding, as well as horse care and stable management.

Members of Pony Clubs may use either horses or ponies for their mounts. (In England a child's mount is always referred to as a pony—regardless of whether it is a pony or a horse.) They may use their own horse or arrange through the club to borrow one. Each member must have a Pony Club–approved helmet and suitable boots and clothing. The gear need not be expensive or fancy, but it must meet pre-

scribed safety standards. Nail polish, makeup, and dangling earrings are strongly discouraged.

A Pony Club education begins with the most basic information and skills. It progresses through distinct levels, from D to A ratings (see box on page 161), up to advanced studies in stable management, horse care, and riding. Members learn to keep their horses and ponies properly fed, groomed, and shod. They are taught basic first aid, correct use of saddlery, safety, and sportsmanship. Some Pony Club chapters run summer camps in which members live and work together for a week or more at a time. Pony Clubs hold rallies, at which members from various levels and chapters can work with one another and get acquainted. They also compete in a wide range of equestrian sports, from eventing to vaulting to gymkhana (competitive games on horseback).

Each of the United States Pony Club chapters is directed by a district commissioner, who is assisted by the parents of members. Parents

help at shows, clinics, and rallies by providing refreshments and keeping score; they also help with fund-raising.

Members must leave Pony Club when they reach the age of 21. Many have gone on to the highest levels of international competition or to begin a successful career in some facet of the horse world. In the United States alone there are over 400 Pony Clubs—and the organization is active in 26 other countries as well, including France, Australia, and New Zealand.

Older Pony Clubbers assist younger ones in all phases of Pony Club activities; the emphasis is on training as well as on practical applications.

A Simplified Explanation of the
Pony Club Proficiency Ratings*

D ratings: Pony Clubbers with D ratings have been introduced to both riding and horse care.

D1–D3: Classes at these levels encourage independence, control, and security and teach Pony Clubbers to ride at all gaits and over fences. They also teach daily care of the horse and safety habits.

C ratings: Classes for this rating promote further understanding of the horse.

C1–C3: Clubbers at these levels learn more about riding, especially about using the aids for smooth transitions. C3 is a regional rating.

B rating: At this level Clubbers should be able to ride experienced horses at all gaits, over fences, and in the open. They must also be able to teach younger members under supervision and have a good working knowledge of horses and equipment. B is a national rating.

H-A and A ratings: H-A covers horse management and emphasizes veterinary knowledge. For an A rating, the highest rating, riding is tested. An A Pony Clubber should be able to train young horses and retrain spoiled ones.
At these levels the Pony Clubber must be able to teach younger Clubbers on his or her own and demonstrate judgment, experience, and maturity. H-A and A are national ratings.

*These explanations are condensed and simplified. Each level or rating is fully outlined in printed form by United States Pony Clubs, Inc.

Kecia Moser, PONY CLUB MEMBER

Kecia Moser is a young rider who has competed successfully in local dressage and combined training shows. In 1988 she earned her A rating.

"I joined Pony Club about seven years ago. I was interested in horses and wanted more than just ordinary riding—I wanted to learn.

"Pony Club made me more interested in the hows and whys. I never would have learned stable management at a riding school or camp. In Pony Club, the older kids teach you how to get through an inspection. You learn from kids who have been doing it for years.

You learn all the little tricks. For example, Listerine gets dandruff out of manes, and cornstarch can be used on white socks—not baby powder; it comes off.

"I was never good at memorizing. But you can't go to a Pony Club rating and recite out of a book. You have to gain practical experience and talk to vets and blacksmiths and ask questions. A lot of people don't realize that their veterinarians are interested in teaching them.

"I had become interested in eventing before I joined Pony Club. Through Pony Club, I was able to talk to people who had evented. I went to clinics and rallies, and they gave me incentive to try eventing myself. Meadow Brook has always been renowned for its riding. Many members have gone on to become international riders, for example, Tad Coffin, J. Michael Plumb, Don Sachey, and Torrance Watkins Fleischmann.

"It took me a day and a half to get my B rating. The night before, there was an oral examination. The examiners ask you questions, but it's more like a discussion. You get into in-depth medical conversations, and talk about how to clean a horse properly and how to take care of a sick horse. The second day is the riding portion. You do a lot of horse switching. You do dressage and jumping—a small stadium course and some cross-country fences. You only fail if you don't handle it well. The examiners want to know that you know what you're doing. You should be able to explain what you're doing and why. The testing was enjoyable for me, because I was prepared.

"You progress from the D-1 level up, so you're learning a little at a time. By the time you reach C-3, you understand the anatomy of the horse better. It's a build-up system, a progressive learning experience. There's no other way you can learn as much. If you graduate as an A, you're capable of running a farm! Very few reach that rating. According to a Pony Club newsletter, in 1986,

201 people were tested for the B rating and 160, or 80 percent, passed. There were 75 tested for the A rating, and only 26, or 35 percent, passed.

"If you don't pass, you feel disappointed and angry for a few weeks. Then you begin to think about the criticism and what you have to learn for the next time. It makes you a more responsible person."

4-H Club

Local chapters of the 4-H Club sometimes offer horse programs for young people between the ages of seven and 19. Depending on regional interests, the program might include English or Western riding; instructional clinics; trail rides; practical instruction in horse care, safety, and stable management; and various special projects, such as organizing horse shows.

The animal science department of Cornell University publishes study guides for 4-H use. These guides outline what the lessons should cover, contain questions for members to answer, suggest field trips—for example, visits to libraries and tack and feed stores—and list exercises in which the member might participate. At the beginner level the recommended activities include: presentations for parents and other members, participation in a horse show as a rider or helper, working on a community project that involves horses, attending meetings and field trips, and keeping records of participation in the horse program ("My Year in 4-H"). Recordkeeping is an important part of 4-H.

The best part of any 4-H project is working with your horse!

Boy Scout and Girl Scout Merit Badges

Both the Girl Scouts and the Boy Scouts offer badges for horsemanship. Candidates can ride English or Western. Some troops organize riding programs for all members, whereas others require Scouts to pursue the requirements on their own under the supervision of a riding instructor and the Scout leader.

The Girl Scouts give two badges: Horseback Rider and Horse Lover. For the Horseback Rider badge the candidate must demonstrate the ability to mount and dismount correctly, turn and stop a horse, post to the trot, canter, and help someone else to understand safety around horses. She must choose and complete seven out of 12 listed exercises.

The Horse Lover badge is based more on general knowledge than on riding skills. Candidates must investigate community riding facilities, visit a stable, and learn about horse care and nutrition. Six out of 12 exercises must be completed.

The Boy Scouts publish a horsemanship booklet as part of their merit badge series. It contains information on stable management, riding, and different kinds of horses. Badge requirements are based on 10 exercises, which include knowledge of anatomy, breeds, saddlery, health, and horse care. The riding portion requires the candidate to mount, walk in a straight line for 60 feet, make a half circle 16 feet in diameter, trot in a straight line and make a half circle, canter a circle on the proper lead and change direction, halt, back, and dismount.

Fox Hunting

Hunting began in England in the 18th century as a means of helping farmers and landowners control the fox population, which killed their sheep and poultry. Over the years it became a British tradition, complete with its own set of manners, dress, and language. It was brought to America by the British colonists.

The object of the hunt is for the pack of

The huntsman and some of the hounds await the start of the day.

hounds, followed by horses and riders, to chase the fox to ground—when he is caught and killed, it is said that the fox has "gone to ground."

The person in charge of the hunt is called the Master of Foxhounds (M.F.H.). This individual, along with the Huntsman, handles the pack of hounds by sounding various signals on the hunting horn, as well as by voice commands. The Field Master is in charge of all the riders.

The hunt begins at a designated spot in the countryside. The M.F.H. tells the Huntsman that he may move the pack to an area where he expects to find a fox. The hounds begin to search (cast) for the scent, and the fox—sensing he is in danger—may leave his hiding place and run for safety. When the hounds take off in pursuit of the fox that has "gone away," the signal is heard from the Huntsman's horn, "tally-ho!" is shouted, and the horses gallop off after the pack.

While they are on the field, a strict protocol governs the order and placement of riders. The hounds are, of course, always out in front, followed by the Huntsman and the whippers-in, who help to keep the hounds together with the pack. The M.F.H. leads the field, along with senior members of the hunt. Junior riders, inexperienced riders, or those on green horses stay to the back of the field.

The hunt staff usually wear red coats known as "pink" coats. Members of the hunt wear black coats (or tweed, on less formal occasions), a hunting cap (or bowler), high boots, a rat-catcher shirt, a vest, and a hunting stock—a white tie that is fastened with a plain gold pin. (The stock originally served another purpose—as bandaging in the event of an injury on the field.) They also wear gloves and may tuck an extra pair of string gloves beneath their saddle billets in case of wet weather. Hunters may carry a sandwich case and a flask as well.

Manners are carefully observed. It is important to say "good morning" and "good night" to the hunt staff, to avoid passing the Master of Foxhounds and to thank him after the hunt, to put a red ribbon on your horse's tail if he is a kicker, to close gates behind you, and to generally be thoughtful and considerate of your fellow riders and the property of others.

Animal lovers who feel sorry for the fox will be glad to learn that today many hunts are "drag" hunts, where the scent is laid by members of the hunt for the hounds to follow and no live fox is chased. Drag hunting may appeal to those whose main goal is to gallop and jump, because the advance planning of the laying of the scent allows for plenty of both. Those who prefer the true spirit of the hunt, with a live quarry and its unpredictability, are willing to put up with a slower pace when required.

A good way to start hunting is to go during the "cubbing" season, when the young hounds are taught their skills. It is slower paced and

Most organized hunts meet twice a week throughout the September–March season.

serves as an introduction to the sport for those who have never hunted.

Participants who are not regular members of the hunt are charged a fee called a "cap" or "capping fee" since the money for the hunt club was traditionally collected in a cap.

Vaulting

Many young people who enjoy gymnastic sports can now enjoy gymnastic horse sports as well. Vaulting, which dates back to Roman times, is gymnastics performed on a moving horse. It was originally intended to develop a rider's sensitivity to the horse's movement and balance, but it has now become a sport unto itself.

Vaulters wear leotards and slippers rather than traditional riding gear. And instead of a saddle, the vaulter uses a leather vaulting surcingle—a wide strap buckled around the horse with padded handles on either side of the withers and straps built in for use in hanging exercises.

The vaulting horse must be sound, over six years of age, and have a very good disposition. He must be willing to accept people mounting and dismounting at the trot and canter and get used to having them move about on his back.

Vaulting competitions consist of various compulsory exercises: the basic seat, the flag, the mill, the flank, the free stand, and the scissors. Then the team presents a freestyle performance composed by its members. During team competition as many as three riders may be performing on a horse at one time. Exercises are judged based on techniques of the rider—not the horse—although the judge does take the vaulter's consideration of the horse into account.

Vaulters performing a triple movement known as the Flying Angel.

Team members performing a double movement during a freestyle exhibition.

Riding for the Handicapped

Horseback riding is perhaps even more meaningful to handicapped riders than to anyone else, for it often gives them a feeling of freedom that they cannot experience in a wheelchair or in other limited situations. Riding may help weakened muscles, improve balance, and give handicapped riders strength and confidence.

Specially trained therapists and riding instructors work with students whose difficulties include emotional disorders, retardation, paralysis, blindness, deafness, missing limbs, and problems with coordination. Medical specialists have found that exercise on horseback often accomplishes more than other forms of therapy in relaxing muscles and improving posture, strength, and balance. Riders can enjoy a feeling of companionship with their mounts and, perhaps for the only time in their daily lives, move about freely, thanks to their equine partners.

In 1984 the International Games for the Disabled held at the Caumsett Equestrian Center in Long Island, New York, included equestrian sports for the first time. Riders from six nations participated in dressage, horsemanship, obstacle events, and relay races. Entries were divided into two categories: C.P. (for cerebral palsy) and L.A. (*les autres*—French for "the others," to denote a variety of disabilities). Riders who were unable to walk without assistance guided horses capably through precise dressage tests, and a blind rider used a battery-powered headset so that her instructor could give her directions as she negotiated a course of obstacles. Judges took the handicaps into consideration without sacrificing the important principles of riding. Judging the handicapped requires an understanding of both the sport and the participant. If a rider is abrupt in the use of his hands, for example, the judge has to determine whether it is something that cannot be controlled before penalizing the rider.

Many countries have riding programs for the handicapped, some government funded and others relying on private donations. In the United States riding for the handicapped is primarily privately funded and is headed by the National Foundation for Happy Horsemanship for the Handicapped, Inc.; North American Riding for the Handicapped Association, Inc.; and various smaller organizations around the country. These organizations establish regulations and guidelines, set up riding programs and competitions, and educate the public.

A Note About Safety

This is not a "how-to" book. As such, it cannot properly address all the issues concerning safety practices around horses. All those involved in the preparation of this book want to emphasize that ANY ACTIVITY INVOLVING A REAL, LIVE HORSE OR PONY IS POTENTIALLY HAZARDOUS whether you are on the ground or in the saddle. It is important to seek out qualified individuals who can teach you safe handling and riding practices before attempting any activity on your own. The United States Pony Clubs, Inc., has created a USPC Safety Information Packet for their members that can be purchased by writing to them at 893 S. Matlack Street, Suite 110, West Chester, Pennsylvania, 19382-4913, or calling (215) 436-0300.

Horse-Related Associations

American Horse Shows Association
220 East 42nd Street
New York, NY 10017-5806
(212) 972-2472

National 4-H Club
7100 Connecticut Avenue
Chevy Chase, MD 20815
(301) 656-9000

United States Combined Training Association
292 Bridge Street
South Hamilton, MA 01982
(617) 468-7133

United States Dressage Federation
P.O. Box 80668
Lincoln, NB 68501
(402) 477-1251

United States Equestrian Team
Box 240
Gladstone, NJ 07932
(201) 234-0155

United States Pony Clubs, Inc.
893 S. Matlack Street, Suite 110
West Chester, PA 19382
(215) 436-0300

Horse Protection and Adoption Agencies

American Horse Council
1700 K Street N.W.
Suite 300
Washington, D.C. 20006
(202) 296-4031

American Horse Protection Association
1000 29th Street N.W.
Suite T-100
Washington, D.C. 20007
(202) 965-0500

American Humane Association
9725 E. Hampton Avenue
Denver, CO 80231
(303) 695-0811

Humane Organization for Retired
Standardbred Equines (H.O.R.S.E.)
Box 88
Church Road, VA 23833
(804) 265-5257

Humane Society of the United States
2100 L Street N.W.
Washington, D.C. 20037
(202) 452-1100

International Society for the
Protection of Mustangs and Burros
11790 Deodar Way
Reno, NV 89506
(702) 972-1989

Breed Registries

American Association of Breeders
of Holsteiner Horses, Inc.
Woodman Road
S. Hampton, NH 03827
(603) 394-7605 or (617) 388-9242

American Connemara Pony Society
HoshieKon Farm
P.O. Box 513
Goshen, CT 06756
(203) 491-3521

American Hackney Horse Society
302 West Clare
P.O. Box 174
Pittsfield, IL 62363
(217) 285-2472

The American Hanoverian Society, Inc.
831 Bay Avenue
Suite 2-E
Capitola, CA 95010
(408) 476-4461

American Miniature Horse Registry
P.O. Box 3415
Peoria, IL 61614
(309) 691-9661

American Morgan Horse Association, Inc.
P.O. Box 1
Westmoreland, NY 13490
(315) 735-7522

American Quarter Horse Association
2701 I-40 East
Amarillo, TX 79168
(806) 376-4811

American Saddlebred Horse Association, Inc.
4093 Ironworks Pike
Lexington, KY 40511
(606) 259-2742

American Shetland Pony Club
P.O. Box 3415
Peoria, IL 61614
(309) 691-9661

American Shire Horse Association
1687 N.E. 56th Street
Altoona, IA 50009
(515) 265-7676

American Trakehner Association, Inc.
5008 Pine Creek Drive, Suite B
Westerville, OH 43081
(614) 895-1466

Appaloosa Horse Club, Inc.
P.O. Box 8403
Moscow, ID 83843
(208) 882-5578

Arabian Horse Registry of America, Inc.
1200 Zuni Street
Westminster, CO 80234
(303) 450-4748

Belgian Draft Horse Corporation of America
P.O. Box 335
Wabash, IN 46992
(219) 563-3205

Clydesdale Breeders of the U.S.A.
17378 Kelley Road
Pecatonica, IL 61063
(815) 247-8780

Foundation for the Preservation and
Protection of the Przewalski Horse
Animal Science Building
Virginia Tech
Blacksburg, VA 24061
(703) 961-5252

International American
Albino Association
P.O. Box 79
Crabtree, OR 97335
(503) 926-2413

International Andalusian Horse Association
256 So. Robertson, #9378F
Beverly Hills, CA 90211
(818) 706-0625

The Jockey Club (Thoroughbred)
380 Madison Avenue
New York, NY 10017
(212) 599-1919

Palomino Horse Association, Inc.
P.O. Box 324
Jefferson City, MO 65102

Percheron Horse Association of America
P.O. Box 141
Federicktown, OH 43022
(614) 694-3602

Pinto Horse Association of America, Inc.
7525 Mission Gorge Road, Suite C
San Diego, CA 92120
(619) 286-1570

Pony of the Americas Club
5240 Elmwood Avenue
Indianapolis, IN 46203
(317) 788-0107

Tennessee Walking Horse Breeders'
and Exhibitors' Association
P.O. Box 286
Lewisburg, TN 37091
(615) 359-1574

U.S. Icelandic Horse Federation
38 Park Street
Montclair, NJ 07042
(201) 783-3429

United States Lipizzan Registry
3917 Riverside Drive #9177
Burbank, CA 91505

United States Trotting Association
(Standardbred)
750 Michigan Avenue
Columbus, OH 43215
(614) 224-2291

Welsh Pony and Cob Society of America
P.O. Box 2977
Winchester, VA 22601
(703) 667-6195

Bibliography

Conrad, Charles W.
Understanding Horse Psychology
Farnham Horse Library, 1989
Omaha, Nebraska

Dossenbach, Monique, and Hans D.
The Noble Horse
G. K. Hall & Co., 1983
Boston, Massachusetts

Felton, W. Sidney
Masters of Equitation
J. A. Allen & Co. Ltd., 1962
London, England

Girón Tena, Francisco
El Caballo en España
Ministry of Information and Tourism
Madrid, Spain

Gordon-Watson, Mary
Handbook of Riding
Alfred A. Knopf, Inc., 1982
New York, New York

Hanson-Boylen, Christilot
Horse Lover's Diary
Random House and Madison Press Ltd., 1983
New York, New York, and Ontario, Canada

Kidd, Jane
An Illustrated Guide to Horse and Pony Care
Salamander Books Ltd., 1981
New York, New York

Le Metayer, Pierre-Charles
Le Livre du Cheval
Gallimard, 1976
Paris, France

Reddick, Kate
Horses
Bantam Books, 1976
New York, New York

Sigurjønsson Ijøsmyadari, Sigurgeir
Hestar
YSJA, 1985
Reykjavík, Iceland

Silver, Caroline
Guide to the Horses of the World
Exeter Books, 1976
New York, New York

Starkey, Jane
Horse Sense
Sterling Publishing Co., 1981
New York, New York

Summerhays, R. S.
Encyclopedia for Horsemen
Frederick Warne & Co. Ltd., 1952
London, England

Index

Photograph Credits

American Museum of Natural History, pages 3, 7; Animal Photography, 37, 38, 39, 40, 41, 42, 43, 44, 45 (top), 46, 47, 48, 49, 50, 51 (left); Robin Augustadt, 170; Austrian National Tourist Office, 91; George Ballard, 16 (right column, center); British Information Services, 105 (top); Richard Brown, 11, 21, 36, 52, 63, 102, 103, 108 (bottom), 164; John Bryson (Image Bank), 110; Harold Campton, 150; Dan Coffey (Image Bank), 111; Bob Coglianese (New York Racing Association), 124; Culver Pictures, 9, 10; Alice Debany, 57; Joyce de Mol, 96, 98, 140; Bertalan de Némethy, 138; Mrs. Isabel de Szinay, 98; Joseph Diorio (Equine Images), 23; Tim Farley, 108 (top); Cliff Feulner, (Image Bank), frontispiece; Jennifer Fischer, 66; French Embassy Press and Information Center, 2; E. Haupt (Forschungsinstitut Senckenberg), 4—5; Henry Horenstein, 22 (top, center), 24, 26, 28, 29, 30, 31, 54 (top), 55 (top), 56, 69; John Kelly (Image Bank), 147; Karl Leck, 133, 153, 155; Doug Lees (Equine Images), 166; Mary Luke, 82; Terri Miller, cover, 13, 20, 34, 35, 53, 105 (bottom), 117, 131 (top), 132, 139 (left), 145, 158, 160 (top, center, bottom left), 162, 167; Fred Newman, 139 (right), 168, 169; James Leslie Parker, 22 (bottom), 54 (bottom), 55 (bottom), 60, 62, 70, 81, 85, 86, 87, 117, 119, 120, 125 (top), 129 (left), 134, 135, 154 (bottom), 160 (bottom right), 165; Phelps Photography, 131 (bottom); Louis Psihoyos (Contact Press Images, Inc.), 65; Tish Quirk, 88, 141, 152, 154 (top); Kenneth Rodenas, 93; Paula Rodenas, 32, 64, 94, 121, 129 (right), 144; Harold Roth (Equine Images), 104, 109, 116, 125 (bottom), 126, 127, 166; Tobè Saskor, 45 (bottom); Lynn Saville, 106, 107, 114, 146, 149 (top, center); Susan Sexton (Galloping Graphics), 148; Bradley Smith (Animals Animals), 149 (bottom); Jerry Trapani, 143; UPI/Bettmann Newsphotos, 123; Fred Whitehead (Animals Animals), 51 (right); Jack Wilburn (Animals Animals), 113; Ed Wolff (Animals Animals), 112.